CHICKEN SOUP
UNDER THE TREE

By Ivor Perl BEM

Published in the UK by Lemon Soul.
2–10 Baron Street, London, N1 9LL

Lemon Soul is a registered imprint of 2Simple Publishing Ltd
Company number 08608270

Printed in the UK by Pollards, 2023

All views expressed in this book are those of the author and do not
necessarily represent the views of the publisher.

ISBN 978-1-9993781-5-8

www.lemonsoul.com

This book has been published in aid of Jewish Care, which receives £1
from every copy sold.

Jewish Care is a UK registered Charity, No. 802559. Registered in
England and Wales. Company No. 02447900.
Amélie House, Maurice and Vivienne Wohl Campus, 221 Golders Green
Road, London, NW11 9DQ.

THIS BOOK IS DEDICATED TO THE LOVING MEMORY OF MY FAMILY

My father, mother, my eldest brother David, my sister Raizel, brother Mordechai, sisters Blume and Malka, my little brother Moishe and, last in the family, my little golden-haired sister Faigale, all of whom perished in the Holocaust.

My dearest wife Rhoda, who gave me a family in England and whose love nurtured me from a scared boy into a resilient man. This book only came about because of her guidance and support.

Lord Eric Pickles

UK Special Envoy for Post-Holocaust Issues

Ivor Perl changed my life; he had a profound and lasting effect on how I see the Holocaust.

I first met Ivor on March of the Living; he was accompanied by his daughter and granddaughter. We were on the same coach together. Ivor, with his dry sense of humour and gently teasing manner, is great company and we spent a lot of time together.

March of the Living is an annual event taking place in Poland and visiting various sites. People attend from all over the world. There are people of all ages and backgrounds. Some are Holocaust survivors and their offspring, whilst others just want to learn. There are plenty of enthusiastic youngsters about, making it a more uplifting experience than I had expected.

After gradually working our way through Poland, we arrived at the end of the March at Auschwitz. I am on the International Committee supervising the preservation of the Nazi concentration camp and consequently I am a regular visitor. While Ivor had visited the camp since he was a prisoner there, it had been some time.

We stood as a group on the separation ramp where families were torn apart. Ivor movingly described this moment in this memoir. For the first and only time that week, Ivor looked vulnerable. I walked up to him and asked him if he was okay. I know it was an utterly inadequate thing to say but I was lost for words.

He firmly grabbed my wrist and said, 'Listen, Eric, don't believe all that crap about the birds never sing in Auschwitz. It was a day like this when we first came here. A warm, sunny day, blue sky with cotton wool clouds. Birds were singing and butterflies were fluttering between the lines. The Holocaust did not happen in dark corners hidden away. The Holocaust happened in broad daylight, in plain sight – with the world watching.'

It is Ivor's hard truth that I am determined to see reflected in the new Holocaust Memorial and Learning Centre to be built next to Parliament, at the centre of our capital: in plain sight with eyes wide open.

Ivor, I am proud to be your friend.

CONTENTS

MAP

Mako – *Ivor's place of birth.*
Szeged – *The holding ghetto Ivor's family was sent to before deportation.*
Auschwitz – *The concentration camp where Ivor was interned.*
Dachau/Kaufering – *The concentration camp Ivor was sent to when the Germans were in retreat. Kaufering was a subcamp of Dachau.*
Feldafing – *The Displaced Persons Camp Ivor was sent to after being liberated.*

FOREWORD

J ULY 1999. It seems I have exhausted all excuses to avoid putting pen to paper. My last plea, that my spelling and grammar are awful, was overruled by my family with the remark that if they wanted to read about the Holocaust in a book they could go to the library, but they wanted to hear my story told my way. Therefore, I have no option but to begin my tale.

Where shall I start? Should it be the time when I nearly died working for a bit of extra food? Or the time I stood by the barbed wire looking out to the forest in midwinter, the snow knee-deep, on the day of my bar mitzvah, praying to G-d to get me out of this hell? Should I start at all? I owe it to my children to tell them about their father's past.

Having decided to write my memoir, the next decision was what title to choose. Although a number would be appropriate, the most obvious for me was:

'CHICKEN SOUP UNDER THE TREE'

The reason will become clear later on.

CHAPTER ONE
LIFE IN HUNGARY

W HY did I allow 50 years to pass before telling my story? It could be that having a computer makes putting my thoughts down much easier, but I think the main reason is what happened at the 50th anniversary of Victory in Europe (VE) day. At that time, I was on the board of management of my synagogue. During one meeting, the point was raised that there should be a special service to celebrate the 50th anniversary of VE day. I should mention that I can never celebrate such an event – I can only commemorate it. After a lot of discussion, it was agreed what the event should comprise. Namely, there would be a special service to which the local AJEX[1] would be invited, a Kiddush[2] would be laid on by the women's committee, and during the reception some of the dignitaries would be asked to say a few words.

'Of course, you, Ivor, will have to represent the Holocaust', which was only natural as I was the only survivor on the board. But the problem, as I pointed out to the committee, was that I never spoke about my past in much detail to my own family, let alone to 150 people attending a service. I did mention that I have a friend who was also in the camps and goes around schools enlightening pupils about the atrocities committed on the Jews during the war, and I was sure he would be able to represent Holocaust survivors.

---

[1] *Association of Jewish Ex-Servicemen and Women.*
[2] *A communal gathering, with refreshments, held immediately following services at a synagogue.*

However, just two weeks before the anniversary service was to take place, we were informed that the person I recommended would be in Israel during that time. As it was too late to get a replacement, and we could not let such an event go by without some reference to the Holocaust, there was no alternative but for me to represent the survivors. I had two weeks of soul-searching and interrupted sleep. Not having talked about my past in detail – not even to my family – I now had to bring all past horror to the forefront, and the more I delved the more painful it became.

Nevertheless, the time arrived and I gave my talk, which was very well received. When I concluded, I was amazed at the number of people who thanked me for having the courage to revisit my past. They said they had read about, discussed and seen photographs of the Holocaust on numerous occasions, but they had never heard from anyone who was actually in the camps. The impact it had on them was tremendous, and they told me they would never forget my words. I realised then that I could not keep quiet any longer.

In fact, I have since related my experiences a number of times to groups of youngsters, including two lots of sixth-formers in a non-Jewish public school, who received my talk with the greatest respect. I specify non-Jewish as I was concerned about how they would receive my talk, considering all my suffering has been caused by non-Jews. They asked a number of interesting questions, which was very rewarding as I had reservations about standing up in front of 120 public-school students. Here I must mention that I have received two heart-warming letters of appreciation;[3] one from the school head who invited me in the first place, and the second from the college chaplain who introduced me to the assembly, both thanking me for coming to give my talk.

---

[3] *These letters can be read on pages 114 and 115.*

I had better start at the beginning. I was born in a place called Mako, in southern Hungary, on 4 February, 1932. The area is known worldwide for the quality of its onions and garlic. We lived in a bungalow at Nagychilagutca 17, which I have been telling my family was a huge house with a substantial garden. When we eventually went back to Mako, after 50 years, I could not believe how small the place was. I wonder how we all lived there – from what I remember – very comfortably and happily, at least until the latter part of the war.

The bungalow, which my parents had built, was made from bricks, mud and straw (which was the norm at the time). It had a rendering of a sort, the composition of which I cannot remember, but it was obviously effective against the heat in summer and the cold in winter. The house consisted of three rooms and a kitchen. The heating was from a charcoal stove that was also used for cooking. There was an outhouse with three rooms, which I suppose we would now call utility rooms, where the laundry and ironing were done. The biggest of these rooms was also used as a sukkah,[4] with a portable roof that was raised when in use.

My father was in the wholesale vegetable business. He also had a partnership to grow the vegetables. The custom at that time was for someone to hire a farm from a landlord, without any payment, and to grow what he wanted on the field, with the understanding he would share the crop with the landlord. This seemed to work out quite well; we had a good life. We also had a maid living with us – although I cannot remember where we all slept in those few rooms. As for holidays, whenever I discuss this subject with my brother Alec, he assures me we used to go to Harshfalva, the village my mother came

---

[4] *A temporary structure with a roof of branches in which Jews eat, and sometimes sleep, during the festival of Sukkot.*

from, but I cannot remember ever going there. I have recently tried to trace Harshfalva on a map without any success. As a village that changed hands numerous times in the local skirmishes between Hungary, Romania and Ukraine in the 1930s and 1940s, its name shifted with the boundaries.

It was the custom in religious households to speak to mothers and sisters in Hungarian and to fathers and brothers in Yiddish. This was possibly because the lessons in cheder[5] were all taught in Yiddish, and only boys went to cheder, so I suppose the custom was not all that strange. In fact, being able to speak Yiddish[6] saved my life later on.

We were considered very fortunate to be living in a property with electricity (which was for light only) and running water, although the tap was not inside the house but just outside the kitchen. Most people at the time had to use a well in their back garden. However, the toilet consisted of a hut in the garden with a wooden seat and a deep hole underneath, which had to occasionally be emptied. While on the subject of utilities, I remember the way we used to have a bath, which usually took place on a Thursday. We had to bring in the wooden bath from the outhouse and fill it with hot water heated on the charcoal stove, which took quite a long time. Very often, by the time the last bucket of hot water was poured in at the top, the bottom part was getting cold, and as often as not the bath water had to be shared by two people. The soap we used was homemade – it was very rough but also very effective.

Another thing that comes to mind is that I had to take the

---

[5] *A school for Jewish children in which Hebrew and religious knowledge are taught.*

[6] *Yiddish is a West Germanic language historically spoken by Ashkenazi Jews.*

chickens and geese to the slaughterhouse for the Sabbath. The slaughter method was quite disturbing for me. When I arrived at the slaughterhouse I had to purchase a ticket, the cost depending on how many fowls were to be slaughtered. The shochet[7] then took a chicken, held both wings in one hand and, while he pulled back the chicken's neck with the other hand, plucked a few feathers from it, made a blessing and, after a quick cut to the throat, handed the bleeding chicken back to me. I had to hang each chicken by the leg on a hook over a concrete trough, for the blood to drain away. No wonder I took to semi-vegetarianism very quickly. We also raised geese, which were force-fed by holding them down between our legs, opening their beaks and forcing corn mixed with oil down their throats, so that their livers would enlarge and we could make foie gras.

There were 11 of us in my family – my father, mother, four brothers, four sisters and myself. Only two of us – my brother Alec and I – survived the Holocaust. My eldest brother was David, who always seemed to be away studying. He was very clever and learned – I always wanted to be like him. Next was my sister Raizel, who from what I remember was always handling the family's affairs, especially after my father and elder brothers were taken to the labour battalion. The next in the family was Mordechai. From what my brother Alec tells me, he was very handsome and strong, with girls always chasing after him. And then my sister Blume, who I remember was dark and beautiful. After Blume was Malka; she was the only family member who wore glasses. I remember her being tall with blonde hair and blue eyes. My brother Abroham (Alec) was next. As I mentioned, he was the only one to have survived with me, and he saved me a few times from certain death, which I shall explain later on. I,

---

[7] *A person officially certified as competent to slaughter animals in the manner prescribed by Jewish law.*

Yitzchak (Ivor) was next; there is nothing I can add about myself other than the story which I am writing. After me came my little brother Moishe. The youngest was Faigale, a golden-haired little girl of four when we were taken to Auschwitz. Every time I think of her the real tragedy of the Holocaust hits home, especially when I play with my granddaughter who reminds me of her. To think that she was that age when my family were herded into the gas chambers.

My day usually started at six in the morning, which in the summer was not too bad, but the winters were always cold with heavy snowfalls. It was quite a wrench to get out of my warm bed, which had a mattress made of straw that was changed twice a year, usually on Pesach and Rosh Hashanah.[8] That was not the only thing that was renewed during those two festivals. We also got new clothes and shoes on those two Yom-Tovim,[9] and the whole family used to come together. The rest of the year my elder brothers and sisters were away studying or at work. Anyway, as I was saying, my day started at six in the morning, when I got up, washed, got dressed and called on my cousin next door to go to cheder. At half past eight, I would have a bite for breakfast and then on to secular study until midday, walking home for lunch and back to cheder from two until half past six. I did this six days a week. Saturday (the Sabbath) consisted of going to synagogue in the morning, lunch (which was always a lovely meal), and then the afternoons were treasured for playing various games with other boys, including our non-Jewish friends. In the summer we would go for a swim in the River Maros, which was just outside the town. It was quite a wide and fast-flowing one (there were a number of drownings), but there was nowhere else to go for a cool-down in the summer heat. Nearly every spring the river would overflow and

---

[8] *Pesach (Passover) and Rosh Hashanah are Jewish festivals.*
[9] *Transliterated Hebrew term for Jewish festivals.*

cause flooding due to the thawing of heavy snow. Every family that lived in the area and was threatened by the flood had to help with the damming of the river.

We had three synagogues in Mako: one very orthodox which we belonged to, one just orthodox, and the third was reform. Both the orthodox synagogues were very ordinary buildings, but the reform building was a magnificent edifice; in fact it was more like a small cathedral than a synagogue. As we were very orthodox, we were never allowed to go near the reform building, let alone inside it. I was forever dying to see the inside as I had heard what a beautiful synagogue it was, with lovely stained-glass windows, an organ and a mixed choir, which to us orthodox Jews was anathema.

Life seemed quite normal, but of course when I say 'normal' I mean normal for those times in eastern Europe, where anti-Semitism was a part of life. If one day went by without any verbal abuse, stone-throwing, spitting or window-breaking, I considered it a bonus. On my way home for lunch or back to cheder, it was like running the gauntlet, where the least that happened was to have my cap knocked off my head or my hair pulled. But, fortunately, mornings and evenings were quite safe as it was too early in the mornings and too late in the evenings for the bullies to confront me. However, it was all part of life and, besides, what could one do? Telling my parents wasn't an option and going to the police was out of the question. Most of the time the police encouraged the anti-Semites, so we just got on with life the best we could.

Life was relatively good. I remember looking forward to going to my father's warehouse to help him. The building consisted of a ground floor and an upper floor. To get to the first floor one had to use a narrow, steep ladder, without any guardrails. Carrying sacks of onions and other vegetables was a dangerous ordeal. While there,

I thought I was a help to my father, but looking back I am sure I was more of a hindrance. Either way, I was always very happy to go there. There was one other reason I went to the warehouse to help out, which was to earn extra pocket money. I needed it to buy myself a big torch that I had set my heart on, to replace the lantern I used, with a candle inside, to go to school in the dark of winter. The wind often blew out the candle, and the streets were dark and dangerous, with narrow pavements that were slippery and icy, and deep gutters at the side.

When I mentioned to my father that I wanted to buy that torch, he told me it was too fancy and expensive and I should buy a cheaper one. I started to cry, saying I only wanted that fancy one and nothing else. I was informed that if I wanted the fancy torch, I would have to earn the money myself. I managed to earn the money in various ways, like selling homemade chocolate buttons (made with my mother's help) and lending a hand at the warehouse.

After a lot of hard work, scheming and saving, I finally had enough money to buy the torch. I cannot describe the feeling I had when I held that torch in my hand for the first time. I could hardly wait to use it that night and carried it with me at all times. I thought the best and safest place was to tie it around my neck. Even now, I still have palpitations when I think of the tragedy that happened before I could even use the torch once.

I was late for lessons and started to run to school. As I was running, I remember thinking to myself, *If I fall I will surely break the torch*. That same second, I tripped and fell on my face, with the torch tied in front of me. Not only did I break the torch, but I hurt myself very badly on the cut glass. Can you imagine the pain I suffered, both physical and mental? The tears just poured down my face.

Not long after that episode I decided to play truant and go to the warehouse instead of cheder, knowing that my father would not be there to send me back. However, my uncle – who shared the warehouse with us – was there. My recollection of what happened that day is not 100 percent clear, but looking back it was odd that my uncle did not query my presence. Being there all day, without checking if I had anything to eat or drink or offering me anything seems irresponsible, to say the least, especially as I helped him for a while.

After hours slowly went by, it was time to go home. I hoped to go with my uncle as I was scared to walk back on my own in the dark. Firstly, you must remember we did not have the luxury of streetlamps and it was pitch black. There were always stories of wild dogs and wolves running loose and attacking people. Secondly, I realised that not having been home for lunch, my family must have gone to cheder to check what was wrong.

I hoped my uncle would say I was with him all day, and I would escape punishment. But after walking with him for a little while, he went into a house saying he had some studying to do, leaving me outside by myself. Waiting in the dark for what seemed like ages, I thought I had better make my way home alone. The journey home took me past my cheder, where there seemed to be a commotion going on. Hiding behind a bush, I listened to hear the reason for the uproar. When I realised my name was being mentioned a lot, it dawned on me they were looking for me, thinking I had been kidnapped or worse. By then I really was scared to show myself, but I could not hide forever. Eventually, I came out, thinking that I would take my punishment and get it over with, but as I emerged from the bush they all came rushing towards me, hugging me and showering me with kisses, relieved that I was alive. They took me home and gave me a bath and some hot food. I am sure I was punished eventually, but I cannot remember what form this took. Looking back, it never occurred to me I was causing everyone so much worry, for which I now wish I could apologise.

While I am on the subject of cheder, I remember going to private classes, the reason for which escapes me. Maybe I was not progressing quickly enough at the local cheder. I recall that the learning was much more hectic and extensive than at the local school, but I was quite proud of belonging to that small and privileged group.

Here I must mention one instance that I was not proud of. The teaching consisted of lessons for five days, but every Thursday we had examinations to see how well we had listened and learnt during the week. In one such examination, I was asked a number of questions to which I did not know the answers. I thought I could bluff my way through, but every time I answered wrongly, I got myself deeper down blind avenues. The teacher gave me a sharp slap on the face, saying that even great rabbis do not know all the answers and we do not have to lie, and if we do not know the answer we should say so. The following Thursday, he asked me another question to which I did not know the answer. Remembering the slap from the previous week, I said I did not know the answer. I received another slap on my face, as the teacher said I obviously did not listen properly during the lessons, and in future I should be more attentive.

There was one other school examination I will mention. As I had private cheder lessons I did well in religious studies, but my secular education left a lot to be desired, especially arithmetic, which was my weakest subject. My stomach churned every time I had a maths class. One morning, the teacher asked me to come to the front of the class and write the answers to maths problems on the blackboard. I picked up the chalk and stood in front of the class looking at the sums, not able to answer a single one. The teacher got up from his seat and, with his hands behind his back, started walking away from the blackboard, his back towards me. Sitting in the front row and seeing my predicament, my first cousin mouthed the answers to me, which I quickly wrote down. As I finished the sums the teacher turned around. Looking at the result, he said very good, but would I just wipe the answers out and do it again for him. I do not remember the end of it all, but I think I nearly fainted from embarrassment.

No wonder my life seemed to revolve around cheder, considering I spent six days a week and most of my waking hours there. Quite a number of events took place there. One that comes to mind was the baking of matzos,[10] which used to take place every year straight after Purim.[11] The ritual was always the same. The caretaker had to move out of the premises he occupied for the rest of the year, which were on the cheder's grounds. Then the place was scrubbed from top to bottom and the oven – which was bricked up after Pesach – was opened up, ready for use.

Here it is worth mentioning the method used to bake the matzos. The flour was purchased by the community and allocated according to the size of a family. Every family was given a time and date to turn up for their matzo-baking at the cheder. The baking was done mainly by the younger generation; however, the whole family was expected to come along and help out when it was their turn to bake the matzos. The baking method was quite a ritual. The water for the baking had to be collected the night before as it had to be at room temperature. The whole process, from pouring the water into the flour to the actual baking, could not take more than 18 minutes, so that the dough would not rise.

I look back with fondness to the festivals that I always enjoyed:

---

[10] *Unleavened bread, traditionally eaten during Passover.*
[11] *Purim is a Jewish festival.*

Rosh Hashanah, Shavuot and, most especially, Sukkot (the harvest festival). We always used to go to each other's sukkahs to see who had the prettiest decorations and, of course, to eat all the delicious cakes we were given at every house.

While on the subject of looking back, I remember the time my father wanted to go to Budapest to see the Belzer Rebbe,[12] the leader of the Chasidic sect of Belz of which my father was a follower. The Belzer Rebbe was a revered rabbi with a large following. At that time, when people were unwell it was customary to go to the rabbi for a cure. When you arrived at his residence, you gave him a note with your name and the illness on it, plus a donation. In return, he would give you a piece of straw from his mattress to put under yours and would pray for your recovery.

When my father went to Budapest for a cure, I begged him to take me with him. He was at first reluctant as by then it was getting very dangerous for Jews with beards and boys with sidelocks to travel around, but eventually he agreed. I was over the moon at the thought of going to Budapest, a town where I was told there were buses that ran on rails, houses ten storeys high with electric cages going up and down, inside toilets where water washed away the waste, and many other modern inventions. The journey to the capital, which took about four hours, was a bit frightening. The train was full and, as my father and I were the only Jews on board, other passengers took great delight in abusing us. However, when we arrived in Budapest I was confronted with an unbelievable sight. The crowds, the buildings, the cars, the buses, the trams and the sheer size of the place were too much for me to take in, having come from a small town, where to see two cars in one day was an unusual event and where most of the movement was by foot or horse and the tallest building was two

---

[12] *The term for a spiritual leader within Chasidic Judaism.*

storeys high.

We booked into an apartment on the fifth floor and that first ride in the elevator was just magic, but the next day I ran up the stairs for fun. Never having run up more than one flight, I could not understand why I was so breathless, with my legs aching after a couple of floors; the result of being overweight and unfit. But then again, being overweight saved my life later on.

I was told to pull the chain after using the toilet. I used the toilet soon afterwards (just to see how it worked) and when I pulled the chain the water started flushing. To me it seemed as though the water would never stop running. I had the fright of my life, thinking I had broken something and that the whole town would be flooded. I ran to my room, hiding under the blanket.

This is a perfect time to recount the day I went to hospital. It happened one Saturday in the middle of summer after coming home from synagogue. My brother and sister were very ill, but we did not know what had caused the sickness. I had my lunch, which always started with fish followed by cholent[13] with chicken. Within a couple of hours I started to feel very sick. A doctor was summoned, food poisoning was diagnosed and a horse-drawn ambulance was called. There was a discussion about whether we should walk to hospital (it being Sabbath), but it soon dawned on everyone that was out of the question. I was taken to hospital and immediately given a stomach pump, which was a horrible experience. I had to stay overnight and recall moaning with pain. Everyone was shouting for that Jew boy to stop making such a noise. It turned out that with all the heat and flies, and the lack of ice, the fish had got contaminated. I cannot remember why we did not have ice – it could be that as the war progressed it was harder to get hold of anything other than essential

---

[13] *A type of stew.*

food.

Thinking about being in hospital reminds me of the time I had trachoma, a disease behind the eyelids that was quite common in our town. The treatment for it at the time was quite awful. I was given a few drops in the eye and told to wait in the hospital corridor for ten minutes and not, under any circumstances, to open the eye. Of course, with all the comings and goings I was dying to open my eye, just to see what was going on and what would happen when I did. After the ten minutes were up, I was taken to a room with an operating bed and told to get on the table. Two men held my hands and legs down firmly, a third holding my head steady, while the doctor turned my eyelids up and started scraping away with a scalpel. The blood ran down my face; the pain was excruciating. I yelled out for them to stop, but was told not to make such a fuss and hold my head still as it would only hurt more if I moved about.

After the operation, I was given a piece of cotton wool dipped in salt water and told to wipe my eyes every few minutes. But that was not the end of my misery. A week after the operation, I woke up to find my eyelid was stuck together, and I could only open my eye after wiping it with lukewarm water. But after a few wipes, as I tried to open my eye, a few eyelashes were torn out with a lot of pain. Once the eye healed, I had to go back for the other one to be operated on. I do not know how I had the courage to go back to that hospital.

CHAPTER TWO
AUSCHWITZ

THE dark clouds were gathering and, deep down, we all knew things were about to change dramatically. The signs were there for all who looked and listened, but of course the stories we heard were just too horrible to believe. One day I remember vividly: three Polish Jews arrived at our synagogue in late 1943, telling us stories of Jews (men, women and children) being killed, gassed and even buried alive, by the thousands. Everyone replied that it could not be true; such tales were too horrendous to comprehend, especially on the part of a civilised country like Germany. We presumed that they were looking for some sympathy and extra charity. It was the norm in those days for wandering Jews to turn up at synagogues with hard-luck stories, hoping for help and accommodation. There was no way of confirming the tales we heard as we only had the local newspapers and radio to go by. However, by then, some families, including ours, did have confirmation of sorts. One of the laws introduced (there would be many more later) which applied to Jews only was that anyone married to a non-Hungarian had to leave with their whole family immediately. We knew several families in this category, including my aunt on my father's side who was married to a Polish Jew. I was too young to be included in the discussion that followed, but I recall the pain and anguish that went on at the time over what course of action to take. But there was nothing one could do, and once they left, we heard nothing more of what befell them.

The tragedy we Hungarian Jews suffered was twofold: firstly, to have gone through the Holocaust at all, and secondly, the tragedy that befell us was towards the end of the war. I recall the local population protested on numerous occasions, wanting to know why their injured loved ones were not being brought back from the Eastern Front, but left there to die. The answer the authorities gave was that they did not have enough transportation. So how on Earth did they find the infrastructure to transport 600,000 Jews to their deaths and torture? Obviously, they were more concerned about killing us than saving their loved ones.

As Hungary was a member of the Axis[1] powers, the running of the treatment of Jews was left to the Hungarians. On numerous occasions Germany urged Hungary to do more to get rid of the Jews, but although they were anti-Semites, they did not go to those lengths – not until later, that is. When Hungary could see that the war was lost, it made overtures to the Soviet Union (which was by then on the borders) for a peace treaty. But the Germans found out about the plan and occupied Hungary in the middle of April 1944. Virtually from the moment the Germans entered the country, the situation changed as they took control with the help of the Hungarian hard-line fascists. Although the situation turned very nasty after the German occupation, I still recall some bad experiences before that time. There were quite a lot – but two stick in my mind. The first memory is of my brother Alec tugging at my mother's apron, crying that he did not want to go to the gym, run by the Hungarian army, that all boys over 12 had to attend. The gym was run by a vicious anti-Semitic sergeant, who took great pleasure in being cruel to the young boys. My mother answered with tears in her eyes, saying, 'What can I do? If you don't go, they will only come and take you

---

[1] *The Axis powers consisted of Germany, Italy and Japan, along with Albania, Bulgaria, Finland, Hungary, Romania and Thailand.*

forcibly and will punish you even more.' There were no excuses for Jews not attending on medical or any other grounds.

The second memory is of a Sabbath morning service in the synagogue. In the middle of the service, there was a lot of commotion. It turned out there was a stationary, half-covered cattle truck at the station, full of people, some from my family, wearing army uniforms.

Every able person between the ages of 18 and 50 had to join the army. Of course, Jews were put in the labour battalion attached to the army, to do all the dirty work; once they left home, we did not hear from them for a long time. When we heard that some of our loved ones might be on that train, everybody rushed to the station, hoping to get a glimpse of them or exchange a few words. I ran there along with the rest of the family, but there were far too many people. The train was about 50 metres from the platform and, try as I might, being small, I could not get to the front to get a glimpse, let alone speak with my father. Every time I think of that day, the sadness I felt then is still very clear in my mind. It was around this time that food was getting very scarce. I remember I would beg my mother for something to eat. The reply was always the same, 'There is nothing extra to have.'

As soon as the Germans took over, the edicts started coming out one at a time. The first was that every Jew, including children, had to wear a yellow star of a certain size and shape. Sometimes, we were stopped and the star was measured, to check it was the regulation size and in the right place; of course, there were punishments for those who broke the rules.

The next edict was that no Jew was allowed to marry a non-Jew. After that, we were told that Jews could not be in business with Gentiles (non-Jews). Then we were informed that we could not be outside after dark. Following that, we had to move into a certain area;

it was the beginning of the ghetto. And, finally, we were herded into just a few streets.

Before we had to leave our home for the ghetto (for which we were allowed only one suitcase per family), the head of the family had to fill out an inventory,[2] confirming all the people living there and all the worldly possessions they owned. I managed to get hold of a copy that my sister filled out. What a heartbreaking list it makes, that pathetic list of personal belongings. And one had to leave the house in perfect and clean order. All this took just a few weeks to take effect. Every time an edict came out, we thought, *Well, we can live with that.* By the time we realised what was happening it was too late, not that we could have done much about it anyway. Where could anyone have gone for help or refuge?

It was at this stage that my eldest sister discussed the situation with my mother. My father and eldest brother were away in the labour battalion; they did not come with us to the ghetto. In fact, we never saw our brother again, but I did meet my father again in very sad circumstances. Raizel and my mother wondered whether some of us should try to escape to Romania, the border of which was not all that far away. Although the Romanians were anti-Semites, Romania was still not occupied by Germany. Many pogroms[3] had taken place there not too long before, but it was still a bit safer than Hungary. However, it was decided we would stay together. We had been in the ghetto for a short while when we were informed that we had to congregate on the football pitch outside the town and await further information. We were told that we would be resettled somewhere on a farm, which would make our lives much easier and safer.

---

[2] *Viewable in 'Documents and Photographs'.*

[3] *A violent riot incited with the aim of massacring or expelling an ethnic or religious group, particularly Jews.*

One day before we left the ghetto, my mother was cooking chicken soup. The smell wafted up my nostrils as I came home. By then, I always seemed to be hungry as there was not much food around. I thought the soup would be our meal that night. However, my mother told me we could not have it then as we were going on a journey and we did not know how long for. No food would be given out, so we had to take food for the journey ourselves. I started crying and throwing a tantrum, saying 'I want some soup now', but of course my mother insisted that we would need the chicken soup for later on.

The football pitch we were sent to was not all that large and the whole ghetto had to squeeze onto it. Each family was given just one very small tent for shelter. Ours happened to be beside a tree and, as it was a warm day, and there was not much room inside the tent, my mother decided to put the pan of chicken soup under the tree to keep it cool. Fortunately, it was the middle of spring and the heat was tolerable. The toilet facilities were just a pit in the open with no screening. As for water, there was one tap for the whole pitch. It was at this place that I first came face to face with death; I would confront death a lot more in the months that followed. After waking up on the first morning, I went for a walk around the field. Soon I came upon people gathering around one of the tents. There, sticking out of the tent, was a young couple who had taken their own lives. It turned out they were a doctor and his wife. They must have guessed what awaited us. There would be a few more suicides before we left that football pitch.

A couple of days later, we were herded to the railway station by the gendarmerie[4] with the help of the Boy Scouts (some were boys we had played with only a few weeks before). We were shoved into the cattle trucks that awaited us there. There was a lot of pushing

---

[4] *Police.*

and shoving, with everybody saying that there was no more room inside the truck, but more people were forced in until we had hardly any room to move or breathe. Once the truck was filled to capacity, the doors were locked shut, with hardly any light or air inside. After a while, the train started to move; none of us had any idea where to. We had not been travelling very long when my mother let out a cry, shouting, 'We left the **CHICKEN SOUP UNDER THE TREE.**' Needless to say that the food left behind would have been a godsend later on. There are a lot of jokes about Jewish chicken soup, but, for me, every time I hear chicken soup mentioned, my heart aches, thinking back to the time on the cattle truck on the way to Szeged; that is where we ended up after that first journey.

The distance from Mako to Szeged is only about 16 miles, so the journey did not take all that long. By then, every town had a small ghetto. Once all the Jews were assembled there, they were taken from the small local ghettos to a larger one, to be shipped to various death camps. Our nearest large ghetto was Szeged, and we were held there in a disused brick factory before being taken to our next destination, which was to be literally hell on earth. The ghetto in Szeged was dreadful; with thousands of people there already, it was difficult to find any shelter to sleep that night. It rained all night and most of us got soaked. To complete the agony, there was a mental health facility with violent inmates next door.

We had been in Szeged for a few days when it was announced that the first transport to the new resettlement would be leaving in the morning. We could hardly wait for the morning to come, as we thought anywhere would be better than this place. Little did we know that Szeged was heaven compared to what awaited us. We collected our few possessions and started marching, with a few hundred other people, to the station. This time the German SS[5] were guarding us, with dogs and machine guns. When we arrived at the station, we could hardly believe our eyes at the scene that greeted us. There were hundreds of people – men, women, children and babies – being herded into dozens of cattle trucks; the crying, shouting and dogs barking was something out of this world. We did not have time to blink before it was our turn to be pushed into a truck. As we got in, it seemed that we would be the last to board, but the SS kept pushing more and more people in until there was hardly any room to sit, let alone to lie down. There were two buckets on either side of the truck: one filled with water to drink and the other for ablutions. The waste bucket was emptied every time the train stopped, about once a day. I think there were about 75 people in the cattle truck when they shut the door on us. Once the door was shut, the only light that filtered through was from the small grilled window above, and there was not much fresh air either. Inside the truck there was pandemonium, as people fought for the most comfortable place to settle down, without much success.

It took ages for everyone to be loaded into the cattle trucks. Those who were put in last were fortunate as we had to wait in the stifling confined space for what seemed ages. We all prayed the train would start, hoping there would be some air coming in as it started to move. There was a lot of discussion as to where we were being taken. Many places were mentioned, but none of us, in our wildest imaginations, could have foreseen the place where we ended up, which would become justifiably infamous for eternity.

---

[5] *The SS (Schutzstaffel) was originally established as Adolf Hitler's personal bodyguard unit. It would later become both the elite guard of the Nazi Reich and Hitler's executive force prepared to carry out all security-related duties, without regard for legal restraint.*

It was towards the end of April 1944. I was 12 years and two months old when the train eventually started its journey to hell. I am trying to write this memoir in chronological order, but the next few days spent in that cattle truck seemed to pass in an agonising, endless blur. As time had no meaning on that journey, I shall try to recount the episode as best I can. Some of the events I mention could have occurred towards the end, rather than the beginning, of the journey. As I was only a young boy, starting on that fateful journey, my recollection will be different from that of an adult with a family. While the adults were apprehensive because they had some faint inkling of what could await us, my youth shielded me in my excitement. It might seem odd to say I was excited, but you must remember that, other than going to Budapest with my father, I do not remember ever leaving Mako. All transportation at home was by horse and cart, so the thought of a journey, even if it was in a cattle truck, was exciting for me. However, that excitement soon wore off as the journey got underway.

It was late afternoon when the cattle truck started its journey, and my first memory is of everyone trying to get themselves some space for the night. I remember curling up on the dusty floor, just above the wheels, and looking through a hole to see the ground underneath rolling by and hearing the clanking of the wheels going over the joints on the track. Even now, every time I hear that sound it brings back memories of that journey. I cannot recall this, but when I discuss the journey with Alec he tells me the women and children were on one side of the truck and the men and boys were on the other side. It was all to do with being religious. Funnily enough, religion was a crutch for most people in the cattle truck for the next six days.

Here I differ from Alec. I thought the journey took six days, but he thinks it was only four. Not that it made any difference, for inside the truck conditions deteriorated hourly and even hope was very hard to hold onto. The only topic that we all had in common was religion; that G-d had a plan for us and would soon put an end to our misery.

One incident that sticks in my mind was when the train stopped in the middle of nowhere and someone pointed to the window at the top of the truck saying, 'There is a sign from G-d in the sky.' Everybody rushed to the window to have a look. There were a number of planes flying very high that had left a vapour trail behind. Not having witnessed such a phenomenon before, we thought it was a sign from G-d, and there ensued a long and heated discussion about what it meant. Of course, most wanted to believe it was a good omen. The situation was so grim that we grasped at anything that could make any sense of our predicament.

I find it difficult to put my thoughts down about the journey in that cattle truck. Firstly, too much happened to remember. Secondly, what could have happened to be of interest in such a confined space, where all human functions had to be performed in front of everyone else, and where the smell, the noise, the crying and all the other incidentals were overwhelming? It is hard to convey the horror of imprisonment in such a small space. Imagine the feeling of being stuck on the London Underground in a packed rush-hour train, during a heat-wave. Only you are stuck down there for days on end and you have no idea what the outcome will be.

It was stifling hot in daytime and freezing cold at night. It did not take long before arguments started. As for food, we had to manage with what we took with us. It was not long before we had a death on board. There would be a few more before the journey ended, and there was nothing to be done with the corpses until the train stopped and the bodies were taken out. The highlight of each day was when the train stopped; the doors were opened for the waste buckets to be emptied and the water buckets to be refilled but, above all, it was a relief to get some fresh air into our lungs. Everyone tried to get to the doors for some daylight and fresh air but, of course, only a few managed. I was getting weaker and had a terrible stomach ache. After a couple of days in the truck, I just seemed to float about in a daze.

Eventually, after what seemed a lifetime, the train slowed down and we heard a lot of commotion and shouting by the track. Looking through a small crack in the truck, we could see lots of people with striped uniforms working by the tracks and German SS guards with dogs overseeing them. We did not know what this place was called, but as the train slowed down we could hear people shouting to us in Yiddish (which we fortunately understood) that we should eat everything up, not hoard anything, and the children must say they are older than they are. Although it did not mean much to us, by now we realised that something horrible was about to happen. Looking through the cracks, we could just about make out the wording above the arch the train had passed through. It read '**ARBEIT MACHT FREI**', which translates to 'work sets you free'. When the train finally came to a standstill, someone outside was asking, 'Are there any sick people on board?' We thought, *What a stupid question; after that journey what truck did not have any dead people, let alone sick people, on board?* We banged and shouted that there were sick people in here, thinking they would open our door first. But, the more we protested the longer the door stayed shut, until we heard someone saying in Yiddish, 'You stupid people, stop saying you have sick people in there!' Looking out between the cracks, we could see that some doors were not opened at all, and it dawned on us that those who shouted the loudest were being bypassed. When our door was eventually opened, we just stumbled out. We did not have the energy to get down properly. As soon as I got to the ground, I sat down on a concrete block, not caring what happened around me.

It took a while before we were told to get in line: women and small children on one side, men and older boys on the other. I was too ill to take notice of what was happening around me, but the scene I witnessed as I finally got up to get in line was unbelievable. I know that I have used this phrase before, but the scene that I was staring at was quite unimaginable. Two lines were being formed by hundreds of bedraggled people. Some were running from one side to the other, not knowing which would be the safest. Babies and children were carried by mothers and sisters, with their pathetic possessions in torn suitcases. And all the time the SS guards, with their dogs, shoved and shouted for us to go 'faster, faster'.

As the lines started to move, I rushed over to my mother, who was holding the hands of my little sister Faigale and brother Moishe, flanked by my other three sisters. She said, 'No, don't come with us; go back to your brothers.' I cried as I said, 'I want to go with you, Mum', but my mother insisted I go with my elder brothers. Had I gone with my mother, I would not have survived. And that is my last memory of my mother and younger brother and sister, holding on to each other and disappearing through a door.

As I went back to join my elder brothers David and Alec (my father and my brother Mordechai were in the labour battalion), the line started to move. Ahead of the line, I could see a German SS officer with white gloves on, pointing left or right with his thumb. As we moved along, we saw a covered lorry backing onto one of the cattle trucks. Thinking that the sick would be taken wherever we were headed by lorries, some said that we should have insisted we had very sick people on board to ride in a lorry instead of walking. Only later did we realise that all those people were being taken straight to the gas chambers, without the selection process we were about to go through.

As I neared the beginning of the line, I noticed that the SS officer with the white gloves was directing the very young and the very old left, towards the women and children's line and certain death. There were hundreds of us in the queue, and he was pointing very quickly one way or the other. When my turn came, he suddenly stopped, looked at me, and asked in German, 'How old are you?' Remembering what those Polish Jews had shouted to us in Yiddish, I said, 'I am sixteen', and for a second he pondered, then he pointed to the right. I often wonder if the Hungarian Jews in the truck who did not understand Yiddish had suffered for it.

From then on, life or death depended on such small whims or joining the right line. Once I was directed to the right, I joined another long line of people and waited for quite a while before we started marching. Marching and queuing, always with hundreds of people, would be nearly a daily event. We arrived at a huge complex, with dozens of people in striped cotton uniforms scurrying all over the place, and the SS guards always shouting and shoving and often beating us for no particular reason. We were told to undress and put all our clothes in a neat pile because we were going to have a shower. When we came out the other end, our clothes would be waiting, all cleaned and pressed for us.

We had got off the truck at about two in the afternoon and it was now six in the evening (not having had any food or drink all day), and the suffering had not started yet. We put our clothes in neat piles, making sure to remember all the items we had, in case something was missing later on. Little did we realise it was all a sham and we would be issued with the striped cotton uniform. This would have to last me nearly the whole time I was in the camps. After we got undressed, standing there naked must have been terrible for us orthodox Jews, as nakedness was considered a sin, and men and women were together in one big hall. When we entered, it was bedlam in there, with hundreds of naked people being shaved of all the hair on their bodies. The shaving was done by people in the striped uniforms, who were harassed by the guards to be quicker as there were hundreds arriving by the hour. They were not too careful, so many people were cut and had blood dripping from their bodies. Fortunately, being only 12 years old, I did not have much hair to cut. After we were all shaved, we went into a huge shower room where we were given some sort of soap that smelled of chlorine.

We had to wait until the place was full before the water started to come through the shower. The water was warm, and it felt very good having hot water running onto our bodies after those days in the cattle truck, where we had no means of cleaning ourselves. However, we could not stand under the shower for very long. We were told we only had a few minutes to wash ourselves and, sure enough, the water stopped flowing after a few moments. I do not remember having another warm shower until I was liberated about a year later. Having dried ourselves, we were ushered into a room with a long table and shelves of striped uniforms behind it. Everyone was handed a jacket, a pair of trousers and a beret – all made of this striped cotton – with a pair of wooden clogs.

When we had finished getting dressed, we were told to form a queue outside. We had to wait until everybody behind was ready to join us, and it was a very long time before we were ordered to march. It was now dawn, about six in the morning, and still not a sign of any food or hot drink. We marched for a long time. As we neared our destination, in the distance, as far as the eye could see, were dozens of huge barracks divided by double electrified barbed-wire fences, about seven feet high, with watch towers every hundred yards with machine guns. When we entered the camps, we were divided into groups of 50 and allocated to the barrack that was to be our home. The first time I entered one of these barracks, I was struck by the sight of the long, wooden, three-tiered bunks on either side and the long, raised platform in the middle, which was about three feet high.

As we entered, a man with the word **KAPO** on his arm stood on the raised platform, urging us to gather round. The next words he uttered are etched in my mind for eternity:

'YOU HAVE ARRIVED AT AUSCHWITZ. YOU ARE NOT A PERSON. YOU DO NOT HAVE A NAME. EACH WILL BE GIVEN A NUMBER THAT YOU MUST NEVER FORGET. FORGET THAT NUMBER AND YOU DON'T EXIST.'

Then he asked each of us what our profession was, which he made a note of. Every now and then he would ask a person to move over, away from us, without giving any reason. Suddenly, all that had taken place in the previous few days, and especially the last few hours, overwhelmed me. A feeling of doom overtook me and I started to cry. The person standing next to me (I cannot remember who it was) asked me why I was crying. I said I wanted my mother. He put his hand on my shoulder and said I would see my mother the next day. Somehow, I did not believe him. I felt that I would never see my mother again and could not stop crying. By this time, both my elder brothers, David and Alec, saw me crying and came over to comfort me. At this point, the Kapo asked David to move over to the group that was separated from us and asked that group to move outside. I never saw him or the others again, although we did learn something about his tragic predicament later on. It did not take long to be reminded that any misdemeanour would be punished severely; it happened before the Kapo had even finished his lecture. Two Kapos brought in a man; one held him over the raised platform while the other started to whip him mercilessly. All the while, the poor prisoner was crying and pleading for them to stop. I cannot remember the reason for the punishment, but it was something trivial.

I had better explain what a Kapo was. They were mostly non-Jewish criminals who were interned in the camps instead of prisons and put in charge of us by the Germans. They certainly enjoyed and abused the power they had over us.

The daily food ration consisted of warm black coffee made from chicory in the morning, one slice of corn bread (which I think had more sawdust than flour in it) with a thin wedge of margarine for lunch, and a bowl of warm soup made with very few vegetables in the evening – if you were lucky it had a bit of meat in it.

The entrance to the camp was through the gates that had the slogan, **ARBEIT MACHT FREI**. As you entered the camps, the first buildings were the kitchens that catered for the SS and inmates. Then, as you looked down towards the end of the camp, there were about nine barracks on either side, with about 20 metres in the middle dividing them. Each barrack was built to hold 300 to 400 people, but by the time I left that place there were nearly 1,000 people in each.

On either side of the barracks was a double electrified barbed-wire fence. One barrack had a long pipe, with taps every half a metre for drinking and washing. But we had no way of drying ourselves and the water was cold, and not always running, so not many of us washed. Another barrack housed the toilet – a long wooden plank with holes every foot or so to crouch on and a huge pit underneath. I cannot think what we used to clean ourselves, as we certainly did not have any toilet paper. A group of barracks was called a camp, and there were dozens of such camps. We were in camp number four, barrack nine.

On my very first afternoon in Auschwitz, I was wandering about, trying to learn the camp's layout, as we had been told that on certain occasions we had to go to our barrack immediately. As I was roaming, an SS guard ordered me to follow a group of people with shovels, to clear some weeds from a ditch. I had been working for a while, when the SS guard started shouting, '**LOUS-LOUS!**' When he stopped shouting, I started to climb out of the ditch and he hit me. As the others were still working, I dropped back into the ditch. While the guard was not watching, the person working next to me asked why I had got out of the ditch. I said I thought he told us to get out. He answered that *lous* means to work quicker; I had thought he said *rous*, which in Yiddish means 'out'.

As I was working in the ditch, I noticed the camp next to ours consisted of young children that were all twins – more on that later. Not far from the twins' camp, I saw a big building with fire belching out of huge chimneys. When I asked one of the people working with me what that building was used for, he said it was a bakery. Either he did not know the building's true purpose or he thought I was too young to be told, but I did not believe him when he said it was for baking bread. Somehow, I sensed something more sinister and it did not take long to find out the true reason for the flames coming from those chimneys.

By now I was starving and could hardly wait to eat. All the food for the camps arrived in the same big, round cauldron, on a wooden cart drawn by two people and one server with a metal jug nailed onto a long pole. The people working in the kitchens were the lucky ones as they cooked for the SS as well as for us, so they could have some of the food that was not meant for us. Every day started and ended with the SS arriving in the camps to oversee the Kapos doing a roll call. Each block had to form lines in groups of five. Sometimes, it did not take too long to count the thousands of us, but every now and then we had to wait in the line, regardless of the weather, for what seemed like ages, before the numbers all added up. The first night after the roll call we were ordered into our block, and once the doors were shut we were not allowed out until the morning.

Each block had three tiers on either side, with wooden planks for sleeping. Needless to say it was a nightmare, with hundreds of people shut in one room and only hard wooden slats to lay on. Being summer, the heat, the smell and the snoring were just too much. As for relieving ourselves, we had to climb over people to go to the end of the room where there was a bucket for that purpose, which often overflowed as it could not be emptied until morning.

On being woken just after dawn, our first duty was to line up for the roll call, irrespective of the weather. After this, we had to queue for our so-called coffee, without milk, although, however bad it tasted, at least it was warm. After coffee, we wandered around the camp until lunch, when we had to queue again for food. After lunch, we wandered around again until the evening, when we queued once again for food. We then had one hour before the roll call, and finally went back to the barrack for the night.

It might seem odd that we wandered about rather than work, but the camps where we were housed were holding camps. After they killed all those who were not suitable for work, those that remained were held until an order came from other camps or factories, for a few hundred slaves that needed replacing. So, other than doing some menial work, we did a lot of wandering about.

After a couple of weeks in the camp, someone came over to Alec and me, asking if we were from Mako. We said, 'Yes, why are you asking?' He responded that someone from the camp on the other side of the electric fence was asking for us. It turned out that our brother David was trying to throw a parcel of food over the fence for us – eventually he succeeded. He was the unfortunate one who was taken to work in the Sonderkommando. They were the people who worked in the crematorium, where all those who were gassed were taken. They were given as much food as they wanted, hence the parcel of food, which by now was a godsend, although we had to be vigilant as everybody tried to take the food from us.

What we found out later was horrifying. Everyone who worked in the Sonderkommando were themselves liquidated after four weeks. It seems the Germans did not want any witnesses left to testify to their abomination. No wonder we only received one other parcel from David. After a few weeks, Alec and I were trying all sorts of schemes to get extra food; by then we were starving all the time. One of the stories we thought we might get away with was to say we were twins. As I mentioned, there was a camp next to ours with only twins, which the Germans experimented on, to find the quickest way to increase the Aryan race.[6] When we spoke to the twins, they said they had as much food as they liked and were treated much better than us; hence, the scheme to say that we were also twins. But after a long discussion, we decided we could not get away with it – we were nothing like twins in height, weight or looks, and we were fearful of the punishment we would get if the guards thought we had tried to trick them. So, that came to nothing, which was just as well, because

---

[6] *A mythological white race, believed by the Nazis to be innately more worthy than other races.*

not long after, we got up one morning to find the whole twin block empty. The whole camp had been liquidated.

We were being punished in various ways for practically anything and everything. One particular incident comes to mind: Alec and I were having an argument over something trivial when the Kapo saw us arguing and came over, asking why we were fighting. We said it was all right, we were brothers and we were not fighting. He said that yes, we were, and he would show us how to hurt each other. He told us to face each other, which we did, and he ordered Alec to slap my face. Not wanting to hurt me, Alec just stroked my face, whereupon the Kapo said, 'Not like that; I will show you how hard to hit him!' and he slapped Alec very hard. 'Now you hit him like that, or I will hit you until you do', and so we stood there, tears running down our faces from the shame and pain, hitting each other until he was satisfied.

By now there were new transports arriving every other day from various countries, and the barrack was getting more and more crowded. Every time a new group arrived, we thought, *Well, that is all the room being taken up*, but there were always another 100 people being shoved into our barrack, until we thought we would suffocate at night from lack of air.

There was some consolation in it being so crowded. Every person had to have their prisoner number tattooed on their left arm. The reason I have not got my number tattooed on my arm is partly due to the fact that there were too many people to process. We were told to report one morning for our turn to be tattooed and we queued for a long time. But the SS guards said we would have to come back the next day as they did not have time to get through everyone. We queued again for hours the next day, but this time they said they did not have enough ink and that we would have to come back the following week. We returned the following week and, after waiting for a short time, it was nearly my turn. I could see the man tattooing someone's arm about six people in front of me when the air-raid siren started. When we heard it, we had to return to our barrack immediately, no matter what we were doing, so we did. After that episode, we were never asked to go back again; hence, I did not have my arm tattooed with the number I was given on arriving at Auschwitz, which was **112021**.

Trying to get extra food was always uppermost in all our minds but there were few opportunities to get any. One way to get the chance to lick the food from the empty vats used for cooking the SS meal – a feast for us – was to volunteer for extra work on Sundays (the work was cutting turf outside the camp and bringing it back to the camp for the SS gardens). The kitchen was just inside the camp entrance and on the way back to the camp, after we had finished our work, we were allowed to lick the vats before going back to our barracks.

I volunteered for two reasons: obviously for the food, but also because people had come back from the place where the turf cutting was being done saying that there were women who worked nearby, and some of these women were asking if there were any people in our camp from Mako by the name of Perlmutter. When they answered, 'Yes there are two boys from there', women said they would be there next Sunday and would be waiting, and so I was hoping to see my sisters. I did not know which of my sisters would be there, but of course it did not matter who would be there. I was just dying to see anyone from my family. The next Sunday I was fortunate to be picked for the work party. I say fortunate because most people wanted to go (for the food) and being small, and only 12-and-a-half years old, I considered myself lucky to have been picked.

After morning coffee, we marched through the camp gate to the field outside. I remember feeling a sense of freedom and thinking how I could escape once outside. The feeling of space, after being cooped up inside the camp for what seemed like years, was just too much, but escape felt impossible for anyone, let alone a young boy. We started to work and, sure enough, after about an hour, a man told me to go over to where some women were working. I said I was scared the guards would catch me. He said it would be all right, but I would have to hurry and not stay there long. When I got to the women's working party, my sisters Raizel and Blume were waiting for me. We kissed and hugged each other, trying not to cry. I remember being lost for words and think I said something stupid like, 'Look, I am wearing long trousers' (at home no child wore long trousers before the age of 13). Maybe I wanted them to think I was now an adult and I would be all right. I also asked where Mummy and the rest of the family were. They told me they were in the camps, not wanting to upset me any more. After a little while, we kissed each other goodbye and said, if possible, we would meet again, but we never did see each other after that day.

There was to be a cruel end to this outing. After I got back to our work party, we had been working for about an hour when the air-raid sirens started. Of course, we had to run back to the camp immediately and, once inside, disappear out of sight. The nearest barrack I saw was a children's one and I went in, thinking as it was so near the kitchen I would be able to go and lick the vat after the all clear. When the all clear did come, I went outside and saw the people who worked with me crowding round the vat. I tried to get to the vat, but try as I might, I was pushed and shoved and could not get anywhere near it. I returned to the children's barrack and, once inside, I heard a lot of commotion outside. The next thing I heard was the doors being locked. It was the middle of the day and we knew it could mean only one thing: the barrack would be liquidated during the night. We knew this had happened to other barracks. Sure enough, a few minutes later a doctor appeared, asking us to undress and line up for examination. Each one of us had to pass by him. He asked a few questions, tested our muscles and told us to go right or left. Having had this experience before, there was commotion as everyone tried to guess which side was safe. We rushed from one side to the other. In the end, he gave up, called for help and tried again, with the same result, so he walked out and closed the door on us. We sensed the ultimate outcome and started shouting, banging the door and saying, 'We are very strong and much older than the others', but to no avail.

By now Alec had started to look for me. He knew I had gone out to work, but he saw all the others who went out with me return and wondered why I was not back in the barrack. Asking around, someone told him they had seen me going into the children's barrack, so he came over and found us locked in. He started banging the wall and shouting my name. I shouted back that I could hear him. He asked me what had happened. When I explained he said I must get out of there right away. I said, 'I can't; the doors are locked.' There was only a small window at the top which I could not reach. He shouted that I should try and try again, but try as I might, I could not reach the window. I shouted back to him, saying he should go away, as if they caught us we would be punished, but he would not go.

Fortunately, not long after, we were told to go outside for roll call. When Alec saw me come out, he grabbed me and told me to go with him. I said, 'I am scared they'll see me running away', but he took no notice and started running with me back to our barrack, where we also had roll call. We were standing for quite a while, being counted again and again, while the Kapos were running around looking for someone. I started to shake from fright, saying to Alec, 'See, they are looking for me because I should not have left the children's barrack', but he reassured me that they were not looking for me and that I would be okay. Sure enough, the next time we were counted it was all right. But that night we heard lorries coming into the camp, dogs barking, a lot of crying and shouting. We could not see what was going on, as there was no window in the barrack, but in the morning the children's barrack was empty. None of us said anything, but we knew in our hearts that the chimneys with smoke belching from them had something to do with it. How Alec knew the predicament I was in I will never understand, but that was not the only time he saved me from certain death. When we talk about it, Alec says I also saved him from certain death, but I cannot remember the incident.

Soon after that event, I was wandering about in the camp, when I suddenly froze in my tracks. I could not believe my eyes. It could not be; my father, whom we had not seen since he left home all that time ago. I thought that at least my father and my brother Mordechai were safe, so when I saw him I felt all hope suddenly fade. When I told Alec I had seen Apuka (which means 'father' in Hungarian), he fainted; he must have felt the same as me. My father was not in our barrack at first, but somehow he managed to come to be with us. I cannot remember how he ended up in Auschwitz. I know when we left Mako he was in the labour battalion attached to the Hungarian army. I am sure my father told Alec about it. In fact, during that period, I often thought, *Why does my father not like me as much as Alec?* When we used to walk together, holding hands, we did not talk about such things. It was only recently, when I mentioned this episode to Alec, that he said seeing me suffer broke our father's heart and he felt hopeless not being able to protect me. He did not want to make matters worse by telling me about the horrors he had suffered.

Only now that I am a father do I realise what it must have meant to see his young child in such circumstances, to try to shield him or be of some help, without success. Now, as I am writing this, I feel terrible for harbouring that thought at the time.

Having Father with us lifted our spirits for a little while; walking about together and seeing and holding a loved one again was a blessing. As we had been in the camp for a few months before our father joined us, by that time, we must have been just skin and bone. I remember sitting in the sun, hunched over without much energy, picking out the lice from my jacket (by now we were covered in lice, in both our clothes and hair), when Alec came over and told me to sit up straight or I would end up with a hunchback. I remember having only one shower the whole time I was in Auschwitz. I say I, but everyone was in the same situation.

By now, the Soviet army was getting nearer the camps. The Germans wanted to ship all the inmates to Germany as quickly as possible and destroy the whole place, leaving no trace of anything. They did not succeed, as the Soviet army managed to capture the camps before the Germans had time to fulfil their plan.

The week before we left Auschwitz was chaotic, with transports leaving every day. The SS guards could see there would not be enough time to ship everyone out, so screening for the fittest was becoming more haphazard, as was the nightly clearing of whole barracks to the gas chambers. Examining everyone in the camp to see if they were fit for work was impossible, because of the sheer number of people. In the end the guards devised a scheme: they erected a goal post five-and-a-half feet high and everyone who reached the top of the post would be safe and taken to other camps; the rest were just taken away. How I survived that time I do not know, but I am sure Father and Alec had something to do with it.

One morning, we were told to form a line outside our barrack and the first few hundred people were told to march. We marched to the railway lines, which were a long way away. On the way there, we passed a ditch, with a siddur (prayer book) lying in it. Not having had a siddur in our hands since arriving at the camps, the urge to get hold of it was too much. A few people tried to retrieve the book but, of course, the SS – with their dogs and whips – were onto them before they could get it. When we arrived at the railway lines, we were given a small loaf of bread each and told it would have to last until we reached our destination. When asked how long the journey would take, we were told to shut up and not ask questions.

By now we were starving and giving us a loaf of bread was bordering on cruelty; it took tremendous self-discipline not to guzzle the whole loaf in one go. Some people did, but you did not have to be a genius to work out that if we were usually given only one slice per day, the journey would not be a short one. And so, we were herded into a cattle truck again for the next miserable journey, to an unknown destination. The journey took four-and-a-half days in the same horrible conditions we had endured before, but by now autumn was approaching and we were feeling quite cold with no extra clothing.

The place we arrived at was called Kaufering,[7] in Bavaria, Germany. There were six camps in the area; we were in camp number four. Our camp held about 2,000 people only, but the conditions were even worse than at Auschwitz. The camp was in a clearing in a forest. The barracks held about 300 people each and were built half underground and half overground. There was a stove in the middle for heating, which was essential, as the winters in that part of Germany were severe. But often there was no fuel for the stove and we just shivered.

---

[7] *A sub-camp forming part of the Dachau concentration camp network. Ivor was in Kaufering Camp IV (Hurlach).*

As for beds, it was the same wooden slats as before, but this time it was only single tiers.

By now we were in a dreadful state from lack of food and hygiene, and we were covered in fleas and lice. Although we saw a number of deaths in Auschwitz, it was nothing compared to what became the norm in this camp. As soon as we arrived in Kaufering, we were put to work, which consisted mainly of building a huge underground bunker, although we sometimes also helped local farmers or did other construction jobs. We always tried to be together as a family, but it was hardly ever possible. The ritual was usually the same every day or night (we quite often had to work at night in the wet, freezing weather). The Kapos would do the roll call and tell some people to go to the left and some to go to the right. Every time there would be people running from one line to the other, trying to guess which side would be for light work (such as farm work) or which side would be the safe one. On a number of occasions, people who went out did not come back for a few weeks, or they did not come back at all.

One thing this camp had, that we did not have at Auschwitz, was that on Sundays there would be an orchestra formed from the inmates, which played some very nice music. But even this was heart-rending, as one of the tunes they always played was 'Show Me the Way to Go Home'. I do not know if it was done deliberately, but it certainly made me sad to be reminded of home.

By now I was on autopilot; the lack of food, clothing and hygiene took away all my will to function as a normal person. In a way, we all looked forward to going to work. At least we were outside the confinement of the camp, and we also hoped we might find some food on the way. Occasionally, someone found some bread on the roadside; on a couple of occasions, some had the unbelievably good fortune of finding an egg. But, usually, there was nothing other than grass; for by now we were so hungry that we even looked for edible grass or roots.

There were always discussions in the camp spanning all kinds of subjects, from religion to politics. But the one heated debate I remember was when people talked about when the war would end. And the person I wanted to believe was the one who said it would not be much longer. When others asked him how he had reached that conclusion, he answered that he remembered from when he was a prisoner in the last war that the more the captors were losing the war, the worse the treatment got for the prisoners; and our treatment was certainly getting worse by the week. But our salvation would not come for a number of months yet. Death was becoming a common occurrence. It was not unusual to wake up in the morning and discover one or more deaths in the barrack. We knew when someone had died – the fleas and lice flew away from the body and clothes.

One lasting memory of Kaufering is the number of wheelbarrows in the camp, which were always coming and going, with either dead or sick people in them. The dead were taken just outside the camp and the sick were taken to the so-called sick barrack for treatment (where I ended up later on). But, in fact, the sick barrack was just a place where they did daily check-ups to see who was ready for liquidation. Not many people who ended up there left the sick barrack alive. The weather was getting colder, with rain and sleet making life even more unbearable. We still only had the same striped cotton uniform that had been issued months earlier.

The journey to work lasted about one hour each way. It was hard going during the day, but at night it always seemed to be sleeting and it was unbearable. One night, when we got to the place where we were building that huge bunker, I was assigned to unload sacks of cement from the railway. After carrying a couple of sacks, someone who saw me struggling with the load mentioned that there was a big cave round the corner. The cave was warmer, and I could hide and come out when we were ready to go back to the camp. The man warned me that the guards knew about it and I would have to take a chance. Inside the cave it was lovely and cosy, but there were a number of people there already and I had to go in deeper. In fact, I went so deep that I could not see at all and had to feel my way, which was a bit scary as every time I heard a noise I did not know if it was a rat running around or the roof crumbling.

I was having a nice rest when I heard someone shouting in German that we either come out or they would start shooting into the cave. People ran out of the cave – there were clearly too many of us in there to get away with it. So, my hopes for a regular hiding place were dashed, but I did go in there on a few occasions later on. When I did manage to hide there, I was always terrified I would be found out and either shot or punished, but the conditions were so bad outside that I thought the risk worthwhile.

It was not long after that I came back to the camp and could not see my father. When I asked Alec where Apuka was, he replied that he had been taken to another group and had not come back yet. Our father never did come back. We heard later on that he died in the other camp he was taken to. He had spoken to Alec a number of times, saying he wondered how much longer he could hold out. He had always tried to hide that from me. Even at home, he was not 100 percent fit; hence, the journey to the rabbi in Budapest.

On one occasion, I thought I had lost Alec too. One morning after roll call, we were separated into different lines. Alec went to one side while I was sent to the other, but this time we could not run over to each other. When I came back from work I could not see Alec. I ran all over the camp trying to find him. All I was told was that the whole group had not come back; I cried myself to sleep that night. There was nothing to do other than wait and see if he would return the next day, but he did not come back. I wandered about in a daze for about two weeks, when someone started asking people if there was a boy here from Mako. They said, yes, there was one by the name of Perlmutter in barrack five. A boy came running over to me and asked, 'Are are you Yitzchak (Ivor)?' I replied, 'Yes, I am.' He said, 'Don't you recognise me? I am your brother Abish (Alec).' We hugged each other, crying from relief. He had only been away for around three weeks, but in that short time we had changed so much we did not recognise each other. When I asked Alec what had happened, he told me he was very lucky, and his group had been taken to work on a farm where the farmer had treated them reasonably well, which was not always the case.

Time did not have any meaning. I never knew what day it was, let alone what month. The only way I could keep track was by the weather. Winter had certainly arrived; it was snowing hard and, with the cold spell, sickness and death increased. I suddenly developed a high temperature and was delirious for a few days. I craved lemonade as my mouth and throat were very dry. In my mind, after quenching my thirst, I climbed over the barbed wire to freedom. I had caught typhus, a disease one gets from fleas and lack of hygiene, which very few people survived in the camps. As soon as the guards found out I had typhus, they sent me to the sick block. I never understood why they called it the sick block, as we were given nothing to relieve our pain. My mind was foggy from the fever. I had bad diarrhoea and was told to burn my one slice of bread into charcoal and that should help, but I only wanted liquid as my throat was like sandpaper.

The German doctor came to the sick block every day and told us to uncover ourselves. Of course, all of us tried to push our stomachs out to look a bit healthier. We must have looked a sight! The doctor would walk past each person, pointing every now and then, and the Kapo would make a note. We all sighed with relief when he walked past without pointing at us, for the people he pointed at were taken away soon after, never to be seen again.

Once again, Alec came to me saying I must get out of there and once again I said I could not. Not only did I have no energy to walk, but there was always a guard at the door. However, one day, Alec appeared with a Polish Jew we were friendly with. They proceeded to put me on his shoulders and carry me out of the sick block, telling the guard at the door they were taking me to the toilet. I was taken back to our barrack on our friend's shoulders with Alec walking beside us. The snow was knee-deep, and I was shivering from fever and the cold, with only a flea-ridden blanket to keep the cold out.

This time, it was not only Alec who had saved me from certain death, but also that Polish Jew I hardly remember, for which I feel a bit guilty. I do not remember much about the time I had a high fever or how long it took me to get better, but it must have taken quite a while.

There was a rumour going around that we would get some Red Cross food parcels. We waited for a sign, or for an unusual lorry coming to the camp with the parcels. One day some parcels did arrive, but the scramble for them was uncontrollable and only a few people received one. I never found out how the guards decided who would be the lucky ones. I say 'lucky', but some of the people who received the food were not so lucky, and got very sick after eating it. In fact several of them died – either because the food was off or because it was too rich for them to digest, but having been starved for months they could not resist eating the whole parcel in one go.

DOCUMENTS AND PHOTOGRAPHS

#	Item	Qty	#	Item	Qty
1	nightshirts and 'day shirts'	30	24	stove	1
2	underpants	18	25	sewing machine	1
3	women's blouses and nightdresses	18	26	wardrobe	1
4	women's briefs	12+4=16	27	table	2
5	pillow cases	43	28	chairs	11
6	eiderdown cases	18+1=19	29	hip bath	2
7	cotton sheets	1	30	pots, pans	10
8	sheets	19	31	plates	11
9	towels	9	32	cutlery	11 places
10	kitchen towels	6	33	beds	6
11	handkerchiefs	20	34	[illegible]	2
12	jumpers	11	35	straw mattress	7
13	boys' suits	4	36	tablecloths	4
14	men's suits	8	37	suitcases	2
15	women's dresses	16	38	travel basket	1
16	children's jackets	5	39	work basket	1
17	women's jackets	8	40	wash basin	2
18	men's jackets	8	41	~~invalid~~	~~18~~
19	men's and women's shoes	22 pairs	42	bedspread	8
20	headscarves	4	43	candles	4kg
21	aprons	6	44	firewood	3,000kg
22	pillows	18	45	soap	1.5kg
23	duvet covers	9	46	men/women's socks	24
			47	foodstuffs	20kg
			48	farfel pasta	15kg

The Perlmutter household inventory translated into English.

11 személy

Perlmutter Ferencz ˛ELTÁR ˛ makói ˛ Pcsillag ˛ u.

17 sz.a. zsidó lakós által a hatóság által kijelölt területre /get-
tó/ magával vitt ingóságokról.

Sor szám	Tárgy	drb.	Sor szám	Tárgy	árb.
1	háló ing nappali féfi	30	24	törölkely	1
2	alsó nadrág	18	25	varrogép	1
3	női nappali ing	48	26	nekremeny	1
4	női nadrág	12+4=16	27	antal	2
5	párna huzat	42	28	szék	11
6	dunna huzat	18+1=19	29	teknő	2
7	poplán lepedő	19	30	főzőedény	10
8	lepedő	16	31	tányér	11
9	törölköző	19	32	evőeszköz	11
10	konyha ruha	6	33	dgy	6
11	zsebkendő	20	34	jég tárgy	2
12	pulover	11	35	szalmazsák	4
13	fiú ruha	4	36	abrosz	4
14	férfi ruha	8	37	különed	2
15	női ruha	16	38	tarisznya	1
16	gyermek kabát	5	39	ruháskosár	1
17	női kabát	8	40	szalartar	2
18	férfi kabát	8	41	Torba	18
19	férfi és női cipő	22 pár	42	ágyterítő	8
20	fejkendő	4	43	gyerek	4
21	kötő	6	44	tüzelő anyag	3
22	párna	18	45	szappan	1 1/2
23	dunna takaró	9	46	férfi női harisnya	24
			47	élelmi	20
			48	tarhonya	15

The Perlmutter household inventory (in Hungarian).

Szeged Synagogue was used to store the pillaged possessions of deported Jews.
Source: United States Holocaust Memorial Museum

The gates of Auschwitz – 'WORK SETS YOU FREE'.
Source: United States Holocaust Memorial Museum

The life-or-death selection process on the ramp at Auschwitz.
Source: public domain

Women and children selected for death walk towards the gas chambers.
Source: Yad Vashem

The electrified fences at Auschwitz.
Source: The Auschwitz-Birkenau State Museum

Wooden bunks inside the prisoner barracks at Auschwitz.
Source: UNESCO

Ovens in the crematorium at Auschwitz.
Source: Wikimedia Commons

Child prisoners at Auschwitz – taken after the liberation by the film unit of
the First Ukrainian Front.
Source: public domain

The gates of Dachau guarded by American forces after liberation.
Source: The US National Archives and Records Administration

View of Kaufering IV concentration camp taken on the day of liberation.
Source: United States Holocaust Memorial Museum

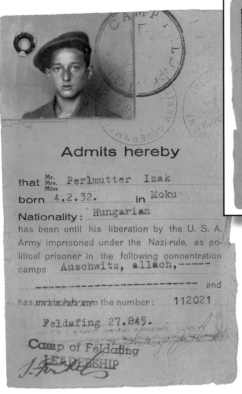

Admits hereby

that Mr. Mrs. Miss Perlmutter Izak

born 4.2.32. in Moku

Nationality: Hungarian

has been until his liberation by the U. S. A. Army imprisoned under the Nazi-rule, as political prisoner in the following concentration camps Auschwitz, allach,————

———————————————————————— and

has on his left arm the number: 112021

Feldafing 27.845.

Camp of Feldafing
LEADERSHIP

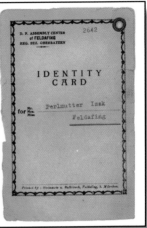

Ivor's Feldafing
Displaced Persons
Camp identity card
(front and back).

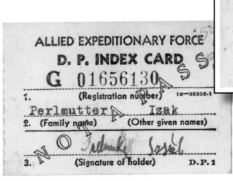

ALLIED EXPEDITIONARY FORCE
D. P. INDEX CARD
G 01656130

1. (Registration number)   16—35306-1

Perlmutter   Izak
2. (Family name)   (Other given names)

3. (Signature of holder)   D.P.1

Ivor's Allied
Expeditionary Force
Displaced Persons Index
Card (front and back).

63

A.E.F. D.P. REGISTRATION RECORD

(1) REGISTRATION No.		For coding purposes
G 01656 130	Original ☐ Duplicate ☒	A. B. C. D. E. F. G. H. I. J.

M. ☒ Single   ☒ Married ☐

PERLMUTTER	Isak	F. ☐ Widowed ☐ Divorced ☐	hungarian-jew
(2) Family Name	Other Given Names	(3) Sex (4) Marital Status	(5) Claimed Nationality

4.2.1932	Mako	Hungaria	jewish	(8) Number of Accompanying Family Members: 1 brother
(6) Birthdate	Birthplace	Province Country	(7) Religion (Optional)	

(9) Number of Dependents: 0	PERLMUTTER Ferencz	PERLMUTTER-Hesenberg Rosa
	(10) Full Name of Father	(11) Full Maiden Name of Mother

(12) DESIRED DESTINATION	(13) LAST PERMANENT RESIDENCE OR RESIDENCE JANUARY 1, 1938
England	Mako Hungaria
City or Village Province Country	City or Village Province Country

(14) Usual Trade Occupation or Profession	(15) Performed in What Kind of Establishment	(16) Other Trades or Occupations
jewish,hungarian,german		

a.   b.   c.

(18) Do You Claim to be a Prisoner of War ☒

(17) Languages Spoken in Order of Fluency

Yes No (19) Amount and Kind of Currency in your Possession

(20) Signature of Registrar:	(21) Signature of Registrar: Date:	Assembly Center No.

(22) Destination or Reception Center: Föhrenwald-Wolfratshausen

Name or Number   City or Village   Province   Country

(23) Code for Issue: 1 2 3 4 5 6 7 8 9 10 11 12 13 14 15 16 17 18 19 20 21 22 23 24 25 26 27 28

(24) REMARKS

Parents and 3 sisters are deported.1 brother in F. 1 year has been in the concentration camps.

MEDICAL CLEARANCE CERTIFICATE

(31) SUPPLEMENTARY RECORD

Temporary identity certificate issued—:

1st	2nd
(25) Dates of Disinfestation: July 45	Types D.D.T.

(26) PHYSICAL CONDITION ON ARRIVAL   (27) IMMUNIZATION RECORD

L.	M.	C.D.	D.

REMARKS

Typhus ex. 1944

Arrival Medical Inspection X/1/45

(29) MOVEMENT AUTHORIZATION OR VISA

(28) Final Medical Inspection X/1/45

(30) RECEPTION CENTER RECORD

Typhus ex. 1944

with 13 years
TAB   Typhus
Small-pox 1 & 7 years
Dipht. 1945

Number   Date   Signature of Authority

Children who left Feldafing for England

AMERICAN JOINT DISTRIBUTION COMMITTEE
LOCATION SERVICE BELSEN - CAMP

Date 6.1.1946

Surname: .PERLMUTTER .... | First Name: .....Isak..........

Previous Name:.......................... | Birthdate: ....4.2.1932..........

Birthplace:.......Makó.......... | Nationality:.Hungarian.......

Present Address:.......................... | Address before Deport:..........

Name of Father:.Ferencz.......... | Name of Mother:......Rosa..........

Information Learned about above person;..........
Left Feldafing for England on 31.10.1945

Ivor's American Joint Distribution Committee Location Service record.
Source: Arolsen Archives

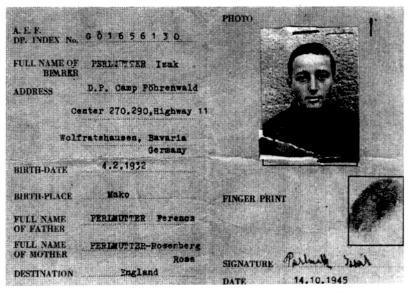

		PHOTO
A. E. F. DP. INDEX No.	G 0 1 6 5 6 1 3 0	
FULL NAME OF BEARER	PERLITTER Izak	
ADDRESS	D.P. Camp Föhrenwald	
	Center 270.290,Highway 11	
	Wolfratshausen, Bavaria Germany	
BIRTH-DATE	4.2.1932	
BIRTH-PLACE	Mako	FINGER PRINT
FULL NAME OF FATHER	PERLMUTTER Ferencz	
FULL NAME OF MOTHER	PERLMUTTER-Rosenberg Rosa	SIGNATURE Perlmutt Izak
DESTINATION	England	DATE 14.10.1945

Ivor's immigration document – issued before travelling to England.

65

Ivor and Alec

David Perlmutter
Oldest brother

Raizel Perlmutter
Older sister

Mordechai Perlmutter
Older brother

Ivor's family home in Mako.

Mako Orthodox Synagogue, built in 1895. The building fell into disrepair after the Holocaust but was renovated in 1999.

Ivor with his late wife Rhoda at their wedding (top left), with Rhoda in 1999 (top right) and surrounded by his loving family in 2000 (below).

Ivor speaking at Jewish Care Young Patrons Dinner (2022) with his granddaughter Lia Bratt.
Source: Grainge Photography

Ivor sitting for international sculptor Frances Segelman in 2018 at Jewish Care's Holocaust Survivors' Centre.
Source: Sam Churchill

HM King Charles III (then the Prince of Wales) speaks to Ivor as he hosts a reception for the Holocaust Memorial Day Trust at St James's Palace, London, 2017.
Source: Alamy

The Deputy Lord Lieutenant of Essex and Ivor at the awarding of his British Empire Medal.

Ivor with his daughter, Judy Bratt, and granddaughter, Lia Bratt. Taken during March of the Living UK, 2018.
Source: Photograph by Sam Churchill, March of the Living UK

Ivor pictured at a celebratory tea at Jewish Care's Holocaust Survivors' Centre for survivors who received New Year's Honours in 2015. From top-left to bottom-right: Agnes Grunwald-Spier MBE, Ivor Perl BEM, Susan Pollack OBE, Rene Salt BEM, Zigi Shipper BEM z'l, Lily Ebert MBE, Freddie Knoller BEM z'l.
Source: Paul Lang Photography

CHAPTER THREE
LIBERATED (BRIEFLY)

O N my 13th birthday, I thought back to the times when the boys became bar mitzvah. Before I was even 12, I had looked forward to celebrating, thinking of how I would handle my ceremony. The custom at home was for the bar mitzvah boy to choose the Talmudic[1] discourse he would deliver to the whole congregation after the service. This was not always on a Saturday; it could be on a Monday or a Thursday, with only a Kiddush after it. But here I was, on my 13th birthday, standing near the barbed-wire fence in a concentration camp. It was a sunny day, although the snow was still thick on the ground. I looked out to the forest, praying to G-d to let me out of this hell, even without any clothes on, and I would not want for anything else. It is amazing how short one's memory is! As I was never bar mitzvah, every time I witness one now, I cannot help thinking back to the day I turned 13.

By now, we felt something unexpected was happening, for it was not unusual to see Allied airplanes overhead daily. In fact, nobody took any notice any more, unlike previously when we had to disappear as soon as the Allied planes appeared. We did not go to work as often as before, the beatings were not as frequent and the guards were almost acting like human beings. However, we still had another four weeks in that camp before we were told that everybody, including the sick, had to go outside. Once there, we were not even counted, but were

---

[1] *The Talmud is a record of the rabbinic debates in the 2nd–5th centuries on the teachings of the Torah.*

told we would be given one loaf of bread to be shared between two people and that, once again, it would have to last until we reached our next destination, but this time we would have to walk there. As most of us could hardly stand from illness or lack of food, how they expected us to walk for the few days it would take to get there was a mystery. They hoped many of us would die during the journey, which is what happened.

By now it was mid-April. Although the weather was milder, the ground was muddy and the marching was heavy going. We walked through a number of German villages. The villagers would come out to see the hundreds of bedraggled and pitiful human beings marching through their streets. One would think they would have taken pity on us and thrown us some food, but mostly they would hurl abuse – and sometimes even stones. However, food was thrown on two occasions during the seven days it took to get to our destination.

The area we were passing through was near the Tyrolean mountains. It is a beautiful area, but I have no recollection of the scenery. My only memory of that journey is trying to keep up with the people in front. At night, we always stopped in a field and had to try to find a dry spot to lie down for the night, which was not easy. On some occasions, when we stopped near a farm, some of us were lucky to take shelter in a barn.

Obviously, I shared my loaf of bread with Alec. After marching for a couple of days we started to fight, each of us accusing the other of taking a bigger portion of bread. We were rolling in the mud wrestling when we saw the boots and rifle butt of a guard. We nearly fainted from fright, thinking that at the very least we would be punished or we might even be shot. So we could not believe our ears when the guard asked us in Hungarian, 'Why are you fighting?' We said that we were brothers and were only playing, to which he replied that, since we were brothers, we should stop fighting as we would soon be liberated and we would be sorry for the pain we had caused each other. We lay there in the mud, not knowing what to make of it. It was the first time a guard showed us some compassion.

By now, we saw many Allied planes overhead and heard a lot of artillery shells exploding in the distance. We took no notice of the shells as we could barely stand upright from weakness. After seven days of marching, we arrived outside a huge camp and were told we had reached our destination, but we would have to wait in the field outside until all the paperwork was ready. We waited for a day and a half before we were allowed in. The camp was the infamous concentration camp, Dachau.

The reason we had to wait outside was that the SS general in charge of our last camp was told to take us to the mountains and liquidate us all, but he was afraid that, as the war was being lost, he would be charged as a war criminal and executed. But the commandant of Dachau did not want to take us in, saying he did not have room for 100 people, let alone the horde waiting outside. The general in charge of us insisted that he was not taking us any further and we would have to stay there. And so, after one-and-a-half days of negotiation, it was agreed we could enter the camp on the condition we stayed on the parade ground, in the open, as there was no room in the barracks.

On the first night at Dachau, we were woken at dawn by a loud bang. Artillery shells had fallen inside the camp, including one that had landed on the electrified fence leading into the open. Some people, seeing that the fence had been broken, started to run out through the hole. Alec, seeing all the commotion, grabbed hold of me, saying we should also try to escape. I said we would get shot and I did not want to go, but he insisted we would be all right, and so we started to run to the fence. However, before we got halfway, we heard machine-gun fire from the watchtowers, and a number of people who were near the fence were killed, so we ran back to the square for safety.

The following day, we heard shells falling all around us and, sure enough, the same thing happened. People ran through the hole in the fence. We waited a little while before we also started to run to the hole. This time, nothing happened, so we climbed through and just ran at what felt like 100 miles an hour, although, of course, we barely had the energy to walk, never mind to run. After a couple of hundred yards, we stumbled onto an anti-aircraft battery. We stopped from fright and did not know what to do, but we were outside the camp and decided there was no going back, so we carried on. Fortunately, the Germans manning the guns had run away.

As we passed the guns, we saw a hut nearby, which the Germans used to rest. We went into the hut and seeing the beds in there (we had not slept in one for over a year) was too much so soon. When we entered the hut there were two Polish Jews there already, but they did not object when we joined them. We were only in there for a few moments when one of them stared in horror outside the window. We all ran over and saw soldiers wearing strange uniforms on either side of the road, carrying guns with bayonets, and walking towards us. We nearly dropped from fear! Fortunately, one of the other guys was an elderly man and he said that it was all right, they were not German but American soldiers. I was still not reassured as I had no idea what an American soldier looked like or why they would be there. Besides, they looked menacing with their guns and their behaviour, for where we were was still the front line. But as they approached us, we saw pity in their eyes and they offered us help instantly.

We went out to look for food as we were starving, not having eaten for some time as the last couple of days had been hectic. A few yards away, we found a dead rabbit, which we immediately took back to the cabin where there was a stove; we found some wood and cooked the rabbit. I will never forget that first meal outside the camp. We could not finish the whole lot in one go as our stomachs had shrunk. I slumped onto the bed and fell into a deep and peaceful sleep.

I am not sure how much time went by but, suddenly, there was loud banging outside the door and shouting in a language we did not understand. The four of us were terrified, not knowing what to do, but the shouting and banging got more intense, and the men outside started to break down the door, so we had to open it. As the door flew open, six American soldiers stood there, practically with tears in their eyes as we offered them some of the rabbit we had left over. It turned out they were looking for some of the SS guards who were hiding. On seeing the cabin with its doors shut, they thought the SS were in there, but when they saw us and realised they had frightened us, they apologised, gave us a bar of chocolate and left.

It was the beginning of May 1945. We had been wandering around for two days outside the camp, looking for food and looting anything we thought was useful, when the UNRRA[2] people told us we would be much safer and better looked after if we went back to the camp. We were reluctant to return, but it was obvious we could not stay where we were. We met other people from the camp who said they were being very well looked after, so we returned and found a lot of medical and other helpful people doing a wonderful job. I weighed ten-and-a-half stone when I entered the camps, at the beginning of May 1944, and I was six stone when I was liberated in May 1945.

---

[2] *The United Nations Relief and Rehabilitation Administration. Set up in 1943, its mission was to provide economic assistance to European nations after World War II and to repatriate and assist the refugees who would come under Allied control.*

The most vivid memory I have of being back at the camp was being informed that we were to go to the bathhouse, where we would have a hot bath and a change of clothes. That first feeling of soaking in hot water after so long, and not being harassed, was really magical. From then on, we would have a bath or shower twice a week. The bathhouse was a communal one where the women and girls showered at the same time as the men and boys, with only a curtain separating them. As I was a young boy, I was often cajoled and dared into lifting the curtain separating us.

Many people wanted to leave the camp immediately after the liberation. The Americans did not stop them at first, as there was not enough food and clothing for all of us right away. We were allowed to go out and search the farms and houses around the camp, but after two weeks we were told if we got caught breaking in or looting we would be punished. Once outside, we had to be careful, as the war was still going on around us. On one of our outings, a few of us were about to go into a big house in a village near the camp. We usually made sure the properties were empty but, at times, when we went into a house or farm the owner would appear unexpectedly. Seeing a number of us standing there, and fearing retribution, they would usually ask us in and give us some food. On this occasion, we were about to force down the door when we heard a warning in German. Looking round, we were confronted with three young Germans pointing guns at us, shouting and swearing, warning us that unless we left immediately we would be shot. There were eight of us; most of us got scared and wanted to leave. One older chap started to argue and it seemed there would be bloodshed, but we managed to pull him away.

We went back to the camp and told the officer in charge that we were threatened with guns by the Germans in a village nearby.

Hearing that guns were involved, he asked us if we could show him where this incident took place and would a couple of us go with him. We were only too eager to take him there, and the officer picked up the phone, saying something in English that we did not understand.

A few minutes later, two jeeps with mounted machine guns appeared outside and the soldiers told some of us to accompany them. After arriving at the village, they announced through the loudspeaker that unless the men with the guns came out immediately, they would start shooting into the houses. Nothing happened for a few minutes. The American soldiers did not wait much longer and started shooting indiscriminately. Within a few minutes, the Germans appeared with their hands up and were taken back to the camp.

I might as well mention here what happened when some SS guards, who were hiding, were found and brought back to the camp for interrogation. Sometimes, the American soldiers would let us know when they were bringing in the Germans, so that we could form a line either side of the gate with sticks and stones in our hands, and the SS would have to run the gauntlet, with us hitting and throwing stones at them. Most of the time I did not do anything, feeling a mixture of pity and guilt.

About four weeks after this event, there was an announcement saying there would be a line-up of all the German prisoners, who would file past us behind barbed wire. We were to point out any SS guards we recognised. They all tried to hide by putting on ordinary army uniforms, instead of their black SS ones. I stood there with many others, pointing every now and then to a German prisoner walking past who I recognised as a guard. Once singled out, he would be taken away from the rest of the prisoners. Standing next to me was a Hungarian, non-Jewish communist, who had also been incarcerated. He pointed every few seconds to a prisoner and seeing that I was not pointing to as many as him, he asked me why. I said I did not recognise many, to which he replied, 'Neither can I, but I am going to make sure the bastards pay for my suffering.' He was surprised that I – as a Jew who had suffered more than him – was not doing the same. I have been puzzled to this day as to why I did not behave as he did.

Inside the camp, the relief-organisation people were doing a tremendous job. We were very well fed and issued with a ration of tobacco or cigarettes, per person per day – the cigarettes got me into trouble later! We were given a new suit each and told that later we would be given material to have another one made up. We were also given a suitcase to keep all our belongings in and, of course, being so young and trusting, I kept that suitcase under my bed. A couple of days later, I went to my bed for a rest and found the case had disappeared. I felt so hurt to think that after all we had suffered together, someone had stolen from me. When I mentioned this to Alec, he assured me that somebody from outside the camp had stolen it, but I am not so sure. Anyway, it certainly taught me a lesson.

After a couple of weeks, we had put on some weight and felt a lot stronger. Having made some enquiries, we found there was nobody from our family in or near the camp, so Alec and I decided to go back to Mako to see if any family had survived and returned. One sunny morning, we started to walk to Hungary. A couple of hours later, we met some people from the camp who knew us. Seeing that we were carrying our few possessions, they asked where we were going. On hearing we were walking to Hungary, they asked if we knew where to go and did we have money and documents. The answer was no to all their queries.

In our innocence, we thought we would just walk until we arrived. They persuaded us to return to the camp, where there was a committee trying to trace relatives who would put us in touch if anyone in our family was alive. We went back and approached the Red Cross, who said it would take about one week to get some answers. We prepared ourselves for the worst as people who searched for loved ones mostly had no success. Strangely, I cannot remember my reaction when we were told that nobody from our family had survived. However much I thought I had prepared myself for bad news, I must have been in deep shock not to have reacted in any way.

Dachau was not too far from Munich, which was already a large town. Sometimes, when I had nothing to do, I would wait for a freight train to go past the camp and slow down enough for a few of us to jump aboard. Although Munich had been heavily bombed, it was already getting back to normal, with shops and restaurants open and buses and trams running. We did not have to pay for most things; all we had to do was show our identification card from the camp and that would be enough. I enjoyed just wandering about, overwhelmed by the place. I saw people jumping off the buses before they came to a halt and decided to copy them. I found it quite thrilling and would jump off sooner and sooner.

Looking back, I wonder how I had the courage to visit a city like Munich without any idea how to get around or where to go, and without any information to go by. One day, I was walking past a cinema, which was showing an American film, and knew I could spend a pleasant couple of hours inside. I had never seen or known what a film was before I left Hungary. It was very dark inside and I sat down at the back. Pretty soon, a man sat down next to me. After a while, I felt a hand on my knee – what a shock! I shot up and ran outside thinking, *Maybe it is not such a good idea to go to the cinema on my own.* Back at the camp, Alec asked where I had got to; it had never occurred to me to let him know. When I mentioned I had been to Munich and had a good time, he seemed quite surprised, but was less than pleased to hear about jumping off buses and he lectured me on how dangerous it was. I thought he was overreacting and it was just as well I had not told him about the man in the cinema.

I am not sure how soon after this the episode with the cigarettes occurred, but as I am on the subject of Munich, I may as well relate it now. I was a non-smoker and my cigarette allowance amounted by then to a few thousand. I hoarded them in a safe place. As money was practically worthless, the only way to purchase anything was to barter cigarettes or nylon stockings, but cigarettes were the main currency. However, this was considered black-market dealing and the authorities viewed it as worse than murder. A person who had murdered a German had a less severe sentence than one caught dealing in the black market. There were always people going to Munich to barter, sell or buy goods. I had always hankered after a gold watch, but never knew how or where to buy one.

One morning, I thought my lucky day had arrived when a friend happened to mention he was going to Munich, where all the black-market dealings were done. Apparently, he had bought a diamond ring from a German woman, which turned out to be nowhere near the quality or carat she had told him. He said he was going to give her a piece of his mind and get her to take back the goods. I asked if I could accompany him and if he could show me where to get the gold watch I coveted. He agreed, but I would have to hurry as the train was due any minute. I rushed back and put the cigarettes in a shoulder bag. Alec was not there, nor anyone who could pass on a message to him, so I left, thinking I would tell him upon my return and show off the watch. The journey was a bit scary as this time the freight train was a flat bed, with no safety rail for security. Fortunately, the journey did not take long. On arrival, we had an hour to kill, so we went into a restaurant and ordered coffee and a roll.

While we were eating, we could sense people staring at us. Suddenly, one of them walked over with an annoyed look on his face. We were concerned as we were the only non-Germans there and being camp survivors, we felt all the more threatened. When he reached us, he bent down to whisper in my friend's ear, asking if we had no shame eating in a restaurant with our caps on and telling us to remove them if we intended to stay. We were startled but, when we regained our composure, decided not to take any notice. However, we left as soon as we had finished eating.

We were walking along the street when my friend started to run, saying I should follow him as he had spotted the woman who had fiddled him. She recognised my companion and began to run in the opposite direction. He shouted, 'Stop that woman – she's a thief!' Eventually, we caught up with her and a big argument ensued. My friend said, 'You fiddled me and I want my cigarettes back or I will beat you up.' She insisted she had given him a good deal and in no way was she going to return anything. By now, quite a few people had gathered around, with everyone taking sides.

The commotion brought two policemen over, asking what the trouble was. My friend began telling them the problem and I butted in to corroborate the story. Before I could finish my sentence, the policemen told me to disappear as it had nothing to do with me. I said I would not go away as I was a witness. In that instant, I saw the policemen staring at my shoulder bag and I was told to open it. When they saw all those cigarettes, suddenly, everything else was forgotten and I was taken to the police station.

I was asked a lot of questions. There were forms I had to sign and my fingerprints were taken. I was given a number on a board to hold just below my face and was told to stand near a wall for my photo to be taken, front and side. Then they began to count the cigarettes. Every now and then they would drop a packet on the floor. I thought, *They intend to keep those for themselves.* But I picked them up and made sure the total was written on the charge sheet, so I could get them all back on my release. Until that point, I was not too concerned as it never entered my head that I would be locked up. As a youngster of 13 from the camp, surely they would feel sorry for me and I would be let off with a caution; but then I began to worry.

Firstly, Alec had no idea where I was. Secondly, it dawned on me that I was being charged with black marketeering. When I asked if I could leave, I was informed I would be sent for trial and if found guilty would go to prison for a long time. I was taken downstairs into a big, dark, dingy, wet cell, with no windows and just one small light. There was a tap for washing and drinking and a bucket for the toilet. My heart sank when I was pushed in, as in the corner were eight young men who looked like typical German thugs. My first thought was that they would beat me up for being Jewish and because they lost the war. I cowered in the corner away from them and could hear they were talking about me. One came over and asked why I was there. On hearing the tale, he said it was not so bad and I would be released before them.

By now, it was late. We were fed hot soup and a slice of bread with jam. Then we were informed that lights would be out in half an hour. I was dying to relieve myself, but as there was only a waist-high partition, I held off going until the middle of the night, when the others were asleep. I felt miserable and lonely and cried myself to sleep. We were woken the next morning, with warm coffee and bread, and told we would be taken to a prison outside Munich, where we would be locked up until we went for trial. My first thought was, *Good, maybe I will be able to escape on the way.* But we were in a locked van and accompanied by guards. On arrival, I was put into a very small cell with a tiny window near the ceiling. The cell contained two beds, with one blanket for each.

Fortunately, my cellmate was another Jewish youngster, from the same camp as me. He was relieved that I was put with him. We talked a lot about various things but, above all, I tried to find out whether escape was possible. He said I should not worry as he was in for the same offence and thought he would be released a couple of days later. I asked him to give Alec a message if he was set free before me as my brother must have been very worried and had no idea where I was. Every morning, the warden would walk past the cells calling out names of prisoners who would go for trial that day. I had been there for two days when my companion's name was called. I gave him a note and asked him to make sure Alec received it if he was released. But I had no way of knowing if he would be and, if so, whether he would remember.

Now that I was alone I felt terribly sad. It was a beautiful spring day. I could hear the birds singing and see the sun shining through the window. I remember thinking, *I would love to be a bird and fly freely out into the open.* Somehow, I felt more incarcerated than when I was at the camp. At least there I was in the open with other people. I felt as though the walls were closing in on me. The hardest part was being alone. All the time I was there, I was not taken out once for exercise. I was delighted when, the following day, they put an adult prisoner in with me.

At last, I would have company! But my joy did not last long as I discovered that not only was he Polish but also not Jewish (the Polish were just as anti-Semitic and cruel to us as the Germans). How would I defend myself when the Jew-baiting started? But, to my astonishment, we got on very well. In fact, he tried to cheer me up every time I felt sad and despondent. The day after he arrived, a warden walked past our cell, shouting that a food parcel had arrived for the person whose name he was calling and would he make himself known. My cellmate asked my name and when I said, Perlmutter, he banged on the door shouting, 'He is here!' I said, 'Why are you saying that? My name is nothing like the one he has been calling and you will get me into trouble.' He assured me it would be okay. The door opened and I was handed the parcel, which contained some lovely homemade cakes, various sausages, bread and some fruit. After the sparse prison fare, it was a real treat and there were no repercussions.

Each morning the names were called, but never mine. I decided that if I was not called the following day, I would volunteer for kitchen duty to see if I could escape while taking food to the other prisoners. Unsurprisingly, that plan was not successful, but as I pushed the trolley past the hospital, I wondered if I would have more luck there. Two days later, I pretended I was sick and asked to be taken to the hospital. However, not only was it on the top floor, it was even more secure than the rest of the building.

On the ninth day, they called out the name of the Polish man I shared the cell with and, as the door opened, I pushed my way past the warden. He said, 'Where do you think you're going?' I replied, 'I am going to the trial.' He said my name was not on the list and I must return to the cell immediately. I shouted, 'No, I was here before the others and they have all been called!' He said there was nothing he could do and tried to push me back. The chief inspector heard the commotion and came over; I repeated my story and he asked for my name. When I said, Perlmutter, he looked somewhat puzzled and replied, 'You should have gone for trial five days ago.'

I would go that day. I thought I had better have a hard-luck story to tell the judges. In my mind's eye, I could see myself pleading that, as a 13-year-old camp survivor, I had no idea what black marketeering was and I only had the cigarettes because I wanted to send them to my family in Hungary. Surely after hearing this sad tale, they would take pity on me and set me free. But I was not certain they would be lenient, so I asked to go to the toilet, thinking I would climb out of the window and escape. This proved impossible: the window was barred and very high, in addition to which the guard stayed with me at all times. As none of my escape plans had succeeded, I hoped my hard-luck story would hold up.

Six judges – two Germans, two Americans and two camp survivors – presided over the trial and, when necessary, an interpreter was involved. After what seemed like ages, I was called. As I entered, I saw those six serious men looking down at me from a high platform. I thought I had better begin my story quickly, but before I could get more than a few words out, one of the judges told me to be quiet and only talk to answer a question. I stood there, open-mouthed, thinking that my hard-luck story and scheming had been for nothing, and I would end up in prison. I saw the judges talking among themselves and I was asked my age. I told them I was 13. They conferred again and nodded as though they all agreed. Then, one of them said that as I was so young, they would overlook my misdemeanour this time and did I realise how fortunate I was to escape a prison sentence. He warned me that if I came to trial again, I would get a long prison sentence. I thanked them and as I walked out I asked if I could have my cigarettes back. I can still see the expression on their faces when they bellowed, 'Get out of here!'

To say I was relieved is an understatement. Not only was I happy to be free but there, outside, Alec was waiting for me. We hugged each other, crying and talking at the same time. He said that on the first day when I did not return, he was beside himself with worry and thought I must have been killed on one of my joyrides. He did not know where to turn. He did not receive the message I had given the boy in prison. Either the boy did not go free or could not be bothered; I like to think it was the former. The next day, Alec had gone to the authorities, who said they would contact the Munich police to see if an accident had been reported. After several days, they reported I was in prison for black marketeering and awaiting trial, but they would do as much as possible to help. The fourth day was VJ (Victory over Japan Day). There were huge celebrations and fireworks, but it all meant nothing to Alec without me being there with him.

Not long after the liberation, we were taken from Dachau to a camp in the middle of a beautiful forest. It had been used to train the Hitler Youth. It was called Feldafing and was not far from the Tyrolean mountains. It was more like a glorious holiday camp. As I was one of the youngest, the adults I shared my accommodation with looked on me like one of their lost children, always pampering me; life was easy and happy. The spring and summer of 1945 were exceptionally nice. Just outside the camp was a huge lake, nestled beneath the mountain, and we spent a lot of our free time on the shore. As I could not swim, I just paddled, but Alec was a good swimmer and he went in the water a lot. We had a lot of time on our hands, to play and fool around.

There was one day I will not forget. We were playing in a warehouse when we came across a huge box of bandages. One of the boys decided it would be fun to play a joke on the adults. I would be covered in bandages, pretending I'd had an accident. As I walked back to my dormitory, people looked at me with pity and came running over to ask what had happened. When I told them I had had an accident, they were horrified and wanted to know all the details. I never expected this reaction and thought I had better admit to the joke, thinking they would all laugh, but they were furious and began shouting at me. Some wanted to spank my bottom and said I must never do anything like that again. I do not know whether I was stupid, thoughtless, or just young.

Soon after that episode, the boys I was playing with came upon a cellar filled with various kinds of weapons, including brand new rifles. I took one (it was unloaded) and imitated firing it at another boy, making a noise as though it was firing a bullet. We thought it was great fun and, after a while, we took the rifle outside, thinking we would play the same game on the adults. I pointed the rifle at a man and he stopped as though he had come up against a brick wall, with a horrified look on his face. I pulled the trigger and shouted, 'BANG!' There was a look of relief on his face when nothing happened, but then he grabbed the rifle, slapped me hard on the face and took me to the camp police. Naturally, they wanted to know where I had acquired the rifle and I told them about the armoury in the cellar. I was cautioned and told how stupid I had been to think that playing with guns was funny and that I was lucky there had been no bullet in the chamber. Luckily, as no one had been hurt they were willing to overlook it this time. Of course, looking back now I see how reckless I was but, at the time, I could not see why they were making such a fuss.

One sunny day, we were playing near the dormitory – digging holes in the earth with a knife – when I saw lots of yellow-looking coins of various sizes. I did not know what to make of them, so I took them over to the adults. They grabbed them, asked where I had found them and were quick to tell me they were of no value. I wonder whether those coins were gold – not that it would have made any difference in the long run.

Up until then, we had not taken part in any religious services, and we felt a bit guilty, having come from a religious background. However, as there was nobody to guide or force us with secular or religious tuition, and never having had this kind of freedom, we made the most of our time by playing and enjoying ourselves. But Rosh Hashanah was approaching, and we could not let such an important holy day go by without attending a religious service.

The spiritual leader in the camp was the now-famous learned sage, the Klausenberger Rebbe, who had survived the Holocaust after being tortured. A huge warehouse was used as the synagogue, with the rabbi at its head. Although the place was enormous, by the time we arrived it was nearly full and there were no more prayer books. We followed the service as best we could, but being Rosh Hashanah, the praying was very emotional, with a lot of tears.

For Yom Kippur[3] we mad sure we got there early, to get a prayer book for Yizkor (prayer for the dead). The place filled up even sooner than before. When the time came for Yizkor, the atmosphere became charged with emotion. As is the custom, the rabbi gave a sermon that ended with the meaning of Yizkor. There was not a dry eye in the place. The cantor[4] who took the service had a beautiful voice and as soon as he began the prayer there was wailing, screaming and crying. Everyone there had lost loved ones and this was just too much to bear. It hit me then that I would never again feel my mother's arms around me or see my father or the rest of my brothers and sisters. The tears poured out of me. I could not stand it any longer and ran out of the synagogue.

---

3 *Yom Kippur is the holiest festival in Judaism.*
4 *A vocalist who leads people in singing or in prayer.*

CHAPTER FOUR
ENGLAND

THERE were a number of organisations trying to help people find relatives or reunite families, but none was more active than the Zionists. They insisted that people – especially children – should not go back to their country of origin but instead to Palestine. As we would not return to Hungary, we thought it best to go there. The problem was that Britain, which ruled Palestine, allowed very few people to enter each year. We were offered other options and, as we had no way of knowing where to go, we went to the rabbi for advice. He said we must leave Germany at the first opportunity.

Being among the youngest survivors, we could choose virtually any place to emigrate. On enquiry, we discovered the first transport would be going to England. We were overjoyed for, at that time, England was one of the most sought-after places. But when the Zionists heard that a few hundred youngsters were going to England, they tried to stop this from happening. Palestine would have been our first choice, but knowing how difficult it would be to enter, we decided to put our names forward for England first, then relocate to Palestine later.

All the youngsters who had put their names down for England were told to report for English lessons in the morning. After so much playing, I was actually looking forward to the lessons. Of course, the organisers had to keep it quiet because of the Zionists. It worked for a little while, but then the lessons had to cease as they discovered what was going on. The organisers had to think of various ways to keep our group together as the Zionists threatened to kidnap us once the paperwork for the emigration began. One tactic was to take us on group trips outside the camp.

One day, we were told we would be taken on an outing to the Tyrolean mountains, and the American army would provide us with transport. The journey to the mountains was exhilarating, and we had a lovely time, especially as the weather was clement. However, as we were getting ready to go back, there was a commotion among the adults. It transpired that the driver was drunk and some people did not want to board the lorry. But as we were stuck in the mountains with no communication with the outside world, we had no option but to take a chance and let him drive us back.

To us young ones, driving in a zigzag was great fun, and we encouraged the driver to go faster and faster, weaving about all the time. Fortunately, there was no other traffic on the road; otherwise, we might not have survived that journey. We could not believe our eyes when the driver suddenly stopped, jumped into the back of the lorry, took the jerrycan filled with petrol and started drinking from it in huge gulps. By now, we were starting to feel frightened, but we had no option but to hope he would eventually deliver us safely back. We all shouted with relief when, after what seemed like ages, we saw the camp. Despite all that worry on the return journey, I still look back on that day with fond memories.

The people in charge of our group had quite a few angry confrontations with the Zionists about our emigration to England, but the time came when all the documentation was ready. We were told that, from then on, we were to keep every bit of information regarding our journey to England secret. It was clear that if we wanted to go to England, we would have to abide by that request, so we all did.

One day, we were told we would be going to England a week

later. But that night, at half past eleven, we were woken and told the transport was waiting outside and we should get dressed immediately, gather our belongings and board the lorries. When we asked why we had been told we would not go until the following week, we were informed that was to put the Zionists off our tracks. The organisers could not bear to think of what would happen if they disrupted us at the last moment. After all the work to put together the documentation with the British government, arrange transport with the American army and make the flight arrangements with the Royal Air Force, it was something they could not allow to happen.

But the plan misfired. When we got to Munich Airfield, three Royal Air Force Dakotas awaited. It was a cold and misty November night. We boarded the planes with a lot of excitement; we had never even been close to a plane and now we were going to fly in one. However, we were on the stationary plane for about an hour and could hear a lot of talking in English, which we did not understand. After another few minutes, we were told to disembark. England was fogbound and the planes would not be able to land there.

By now, the lorries had left and they had to find new transportation for us, which was not too difficult. But they could not take us back to the camps, for obvious reasons, and finding accommodation for 300 youngsters in November 1945 was not easy. By morning an answer to our predicament had been found, in the form of a place about an hour's drive away. When we arrived at our destination, we did not want to get out of the buses, as the accommodation was a nunnery. We always thought priests and nuns did not like Jews, and this being a German nunnery made it even more unacceptable for us. The adults told us that it would be for a couple of days at most and that as we could not go back to the camp we had no other option; they also assured us the nuns would be kind to us.

The nunnery was in a most beautiful setting, amidst forest and lakes. We were astounded at the help and kindness the nuns showed us. They fed and bathed us; we had lovely clean cotton sheets. We spent a memorable three days there before going to the airport. Once again, when we arrived at the airport there was some commotion going on. Since we had left the nunnery, the weather had closed in again at our destination, Southampton. As we could not go back to the nunnery, we would be taken to Brussels for an overnight stay and then fly to England in the morning. It seemed we would never get there.

The flight to Brussels was quite exciting. The plane was a military one with long wooden benches on either side, and we were buffeted practically all the way. After an overnight stop in Brussels, where we were looked after by the Belgian Air Force, we finally left for England. We arrived in Southampton in mid-November 1945.

The Jewish community in England had formed a committee for rescuing survivors and they had permission to bring over around 800 children, for whom they were responsible. We came over in two groups of 400; one went to Southampton and the other to Windermere, by the lake. Having arrived in Southampton, the first impression I had was of a peaceful and tranquil place. The place in Germany we had left was also a lovely spot, but it felt like a graveyard, with hordes of people either looking for lost loved ones or a safe haven to go to.

After a couple of weeks, we were informed that we were to be transferred, in groups of 40 or 50, to various parts of England, all in beautiful areas. We were taken to a manor house in Ascot, Berkshire, just outside the racetrack. The hostel was run by madrichim,[1] boys and girls in their late teens or early 20s, who had managed to escape

---

[1] *Hebrew word for guides.*

from Germany just before the outbreak of war. They looked after us very well. We had lessons in the mornings and free time in the afternoons. They took us on various trips, but the one that comes to mind was our first outing to London, where we had a lovely meal in a kosher restaurant in the East End. There were a few women there who all wanted to hear first-hand the horrors of the camps. *The Jewish Chronicle* was also there, with a photographer who took pictures of a group of us. We had an enjoyable time, but I could not overlook the devastation that London had suffered from the bombings, especially the East End and the City.

One day, we were told we would be given bicycles, each to be shared between two boys. When we enquired if the bicycles were new, they informed us that, unfortunately, due to the shortages, only some would be. When it was our turn, we waited at the gate with bated breath to see if we would be lucky, but we were disappointed when we found that ours was not new. Nevertheless, it gave us great enjoyment.

A few months into our stay in Ascot, two young men turned up at the hostel, asking to talk to the boys that came from a religious home. After a couple of hours of discussion they convinced us that, although the hostel we were staying at was kosher, out of reverence to our family's memory, we ought to go to the more religious one they ran in Manchester. And so we left beautiful Ascot and went to a dilapidated house in Salford, Manchester. The hostel in Manchester certainly was more religious than the one in Ascot. We had to pray three times a day and the lessons were mainly religious study.

Fortunately, we did not stay there long, for the rabbi who ran the hostel also ran a theological college in Egham, Surrey, which was situated in a very nice area. Looking back, I must say all these people who ran the hostels were a very charitable lot. It was mid-1947 when we arrived in Egham. Alec only stayed for a couple of weeks, after which he went to London to stay in a hostel run by Rabbi Korn, who had managed to escape to London from Germany just before war broke out. He found work in Cutler Street (East London) as a watch repairer and jeweller.

I stayed at the college for a couple of years. Although most of the teaching was religious, we also had secular lessons, which I liked very much; the teacher made the classes very engaging. My stay in Egham coincided with the troubles in Palestine, in which I was very interested. I took every opportunity to go to the library and read every paper I could lay my hands on. The problem was that the library was in Ascot, which is a few miles from Egham, and the buses did not run very frequently. Several times, I had to walk one way as I could not wait for the bus. I was becoming very Zionistic and wanted to go to Palestine to join the Haganah (the Jewish underground movement). When the teacher found out, he took me aside and told me that, as I was only 16 years old, I would have plenty of opportunities to get killed in a war and that I should stay at least a year longer to study while I could. I remember looking at him in horror thinking, *A whole year; that is a lifetime!* But he was persuasive and I stayed at the college until the end of 1948.

Towards the end of that year, I left Egham and went to London to join Alec at the hostel in Amhurst Road. I joined the technical college ORT (Organisation for Rehabilitation through Training). We had lessons in the morning and learnt a trade in the afternoon. The trade I decided on was electrical fitting. I do not know why I chose that skill, as I never earned any money from it, but it certainly comes in handy when I do DIY.

Amhurst Road, where we lived, is not far from Ridley Road. Every weekend, Oswald Mosley and his fascist mob held anti-Zionist and anti-Semitic rallies there. I would go with a few friends to be of some nuisance, but the only effect was that I nearly had my head smashed in a couple of times. London in 1948 was an austere place, with few places for recreation. For exercise we went to Hackney Downs, where we played football with other youngsters. At one of these matches, someone suggested we try the Mile End Old Boys, a Jewish club on Mile End Road, so we started going there once a week. Although the place was very basic, it provided an outlet for our energy.

The establishment of Israel in May 1948 was a great turning point for me. For the first time, I felt great joy in being a Jew. The whole ethos of the Nazis was to make us feel subhuman and, after having this drilled into us in the concentration camp, I indeed felt that we were the dregs of humanity. But the first time I saw the Israeli flag, and heard and saw Hebrew writing, my heart swelled with pride. When I saw the Israelis celebrating in the streets (in the cinema on the newsreel), I wished I could be there.

The Jewish refugee committee that brought us over from Germany took care of us until we were able to stand on our own feet. That organisation was situated at Bloomsbury House, in Bloomsbury Square, where we had to go for all our necessities (i.e. pocket money and second-hand clothing). Every two years we got a voucher for a new suit to be made to measure by Burton's, the tailor. Now and then, the refugee committee made it plain that they expected us to be financially self-sufficient as soon as possible. This prompted me to get a job as soon as I could, as I was always hard up for money and the clothes I wore were mostly second-hand. After enquiring about what the best-paid work was, I was told that, as an unskilled boy, the best job for me would be in the clothing trade. With hindsight, I can look back on success, but many times during my working life I felt that I could, and should, have been in a profession and was angry at fate for having to cut my education short.

I was 16 years old when I found work in a firm called Silverwhite as a blouse cutter, and I was a bit surprised when, after only three weeks, they gave me the keys to open up in the morning. I looked upon this as a move towards becoming manager, so I was disappointed and hurt when they offered me only three pounds and ten shillings per week. Especially as they were Jewish themselves and knew my background, how hard up I was, and that I had to pay £3 per week for my board and lodgings, which meant I was not much better off than before. I decided that I must work for myself instead and, after three months, I went into business as a button and buckle coverer. I had no capital to fall back on, nor any experience of how to run a business, so unsurprisingly that venture did not last more than a few months. But the lessons I learnt from it would stand me in good stead later on.

Silverwhite thought I was a worker worth my salt and invited me back to work for them. This time I negotiated slightly better terms and stayed with them for two years. However, I had a burning desire to be my own boss so I eventually set up business as a belt manufacturer with a friend, with whom I shared a room at the hostel.

Deciding to start a business was one thing, but getting the money for the venture was another. I never earned enough to save, but Alec, who worked all the time I was in school, had managed to save a little money and kindly agreed to lend me some. Money was not the only thing Alec lent me; later on, when I asked my future wife for a first date, I did not possess a decent overcoat and he obliged me once again.

My partner had a cousin who we did some work with. After a while, the cousin asked me if I would like to meet a nice young girl, to which I replied, 'No thanks, I am far too young to think of settling down.' I was ashamed to say I was in no position financially to take a girl out, let alone think about marriage. He insisted, telling me I could go as a friend only, so I agreed. One Saturday night he and his wife took me out with them. As well as my friend and his wife, there were two young girls, Rene and Rhoda, and their mother. I was extremely embarrassed, shy and tongue-tied; as one would expect, the conversation certainly did not flow smoothly. However, I felt the family was warm and *heimish*,[2] which was akin to my own background and something I had not experienced since I was with my own family.

Eventually, the evening came to a close and I made my escape with relief, having no intention of taking it further. Nevertheless, I was persuaded that it would be much easier on a one-to-one basis, so I telephoned to invite the young lady out to the West End for tea. Thinking I was taking out Rene, she asked whether I minded if her sister came also. I was too shy and polite to say no, but was disappointed that Rhoda would be there too. During the conversation, I realised Rhoda was the one I was supposed to go out with in the first place, as she was my age, with Rene being two years older. We all had an enjoyable evening and I decided to ask Rhoda out again, hoping this time she would come by herself. Not that I did not like Rene – in fact, I came to admire her a lot later on – but three was a crowd. Many a time in later life, with tongue in cheek, Rene would remark that I could have married her.

The Festival of Britain had opened at Battersea Park not long before, so Rhoda and I decided to go there. We had an enjoyable time and got on very well. I remember we were so immersed in our conversation that we went three stops past our destination on our return home. After that first date, I could not wait for the

---

2 *Yiddish word used to describe things that are homely or familiar.*

weekend to come along and for us to go out again. Meeting Rhoda changed my life completely. Not only because of marriage but, just as importantly, I acquired a warm and loving family and got on very well with Rhoda's brother and two sisters. The husband of one of Rhoda's friends also became my business partner. We ran a successful clothing-manufacturing company for the next 35 years, which my son-in-law took over after my retirement.

Rhoda and I courted for a couple of years before deciding to get married. I felt that, as I had my own business, I should earn at least as much as she did, so I decided to give myself and my partner a rise from £5 to the princely sum of £6 a week– the sum that Rhoda earned.

We got married on 18 January, 1953 at Shoreditch Town Hall. When I look back, I am thankful that Rhoda's parents accepted me into the family, considering I had very little to offer their daughter. They could obviously see a bright future for us. I must say they organised a very nice wedding, with Rhoda's brother hiring the wedding car and acting as chauffeur. He also played Mendelssohn's 'Wedding March' from a gramophone record for our entrance to the chuppah.[3] Our honeymoon was at the Ambassador Hotel in Bournemouth, and we had to take our ration books with us. We have been happily married for 47 years. We have four children and six grandchildren, who were all named after lost loved ones and who have brought us great joy and *nachas*.[4]

I always felt very strongly that I would not return to my birthplace, but Alec and the family were quite persuasive about a visit to Hungary. So, in May 1992, Rhoda, Alec and three of our four

---

[3] *Canopy under which Jewish couples stand during the wedding ceremony.*
[4] *Yiddish word meaning 'proud pleasure' – particularly from the achievements of a child.*

children, together with our son David's wife Ruth, flew with me to Budapest. There, we stayed in a wonderful hotel with hot sulphur baths, before hiring a minibus to travel the 150 miles to Mako.

We first went to the house where we had been brought up. What memories resurfaced when we saw, coming towards us, a horse and cart laden with hay! This was just like the ones we used to grab onto from behind for a free ride, with the driver flicking his whip to dislodge us. Alec's Hungarian was non-existent, while mine was extremely poor. We approached the house, the inside of which had been modernised. Goodness knows what the woman who lived there thought of this crowd of people congregating outside! When she came to the door, we somehow managed to make her understand that we used to live there. With some hesitation, she let us in through the garden gate. We were astounded to see this tiny garden, which I had remembered as being the size of an orchard, with apricot, peach, pear and apple trees. Those trees were still there, but there was just one of each variety. The rooms were just as small. The outhouse – which used to have no roof and where not only my family but also our cousins from next door used to celebrate Sukkot – was now a garage.

Our next port of call was the cemetery, which was just outside the town. Surprisingly, one section of it was in good order. We learnt that a Hungarian, who was now living in America, paid to have it looked after. We knew our grandparents were buried in the religious section, which was very unkempt. We tried to find the inscribed headstones, which was difficult as the writing was only in Hebrew, whereas in the modern section it was in both Hungarian and Hebrew. Although my Hebrew is quite good, I could not find them. Alec was very excited to see and visit all these places from our past, but I am afraid I was affected in a different way. I felt a strange reluctance to be there and wanted to escape as quickly as possible.

After leaving the cemetery, we managed to find the main synagogue, which had fallen almost into ruin. Opposite were the classrooms I had attended, still with desks and chairs lying around. There was a note on the door of the synagogue which gave an address to pick up the key, but I could take no more and hustled everybody away to the hotel. We stayed overnight in the next town, Szeged (where we had been taken before being transported to Auschwitz). The following day, we visited the synagogue in Szeged, which is the most beautiful in the whole of Europe – a miniature cathedral! It certainly lived up to its reputation, with its beautiful stained-glass windows and huge, blue-domed ceiling. How it had not been destroyed by the Nazis I do not know. There was a massive stone wall at the entrance, with the names of the Jews from Szeged who perished in the Holocaust. The first name was Hannah, which is the name our son and daughter-in-law decided to give their daughter.

Having returned to our hotel in Budapest, I felt dreadfully upset about running away, especially as Alec had wanted to visit the area in more depth. As we had come all that distance and may never return, I persuaded Alec to hire a taxi for just the two of us to return to Mako. This time, we saw where our old school was and managed to get inside the synagogue, where we took videos to show the family. Even the crumbling old siddurs (prayer books) were still there!

I am often asked what it felt like to go back to Mako after all those years. I can never express my thoughts or quite what it meant. I can only describe it as a huge burden having been lifted from my shoulders. The next journey back would certainly hold no fear for me.

Note: The first Jews settled in Mako in 1740 and by 1940 there were 1150 Jews, of which only 350 survived. The renowned journalist and publisher Joseph Pulitzer was born in Mako.

EPILOGUE

January 2000

NOW that I have finished my story, I can look back and decide whether the exercise was as therapeutic as I was assured it would be. The thought uppermost in my mind has always been, *Is there any useful purpose in an individual (as opposed to historians) recounting their story about the Holocaust?* Everybody who reads my tale assures me that not only is it useful but it is also every survivor's duty to record these tragic events; especially now that there is a trial going on about a right-wing author, who is denying the Holocaust ever occurred.[1]

Yes, I can say that telling my story has helped me in some ways. But delving into the past has also brought back a lot of pain. The biggest surprise I had while writing this story was the huge interest shown by everyone who read the first part. I had no intention of turning this into a book. It was meant purely as a legacy for my immediate family. Initially, I was only going to relate my experiences up to the liberation at Dachau. But I was urged by all who had read my story to write not only the next episode but also right up to the present time. They were curious as to whether this tale had a happy ending, which thank G-d it does.

After completion, it was suggested that I turn my story into a book,

---

[1] *Holocaust denier David Irving lost his libel case, which served only to draw attention to the undisputable horrors of the Holocaust.*

with accompanying photographs. I must thank my good friend Martin for all his input in making this possible.

January 2023

Twenty-three years have gone by since I wrote down my story. Life has changed a lot in that time. My brother Alec passed away from cancer, which was an extremely difficult time in my life. I had to say goodbye to the only surviving member of the Perlmutter family; to the brother I grew up with in England. I had to say goodbye to not only my best friend but also the man who saved me from certain death many times. I owe everything to him, because without him I would not be here today.

My dear wife Rhoda sadly passed away in January 2016 from dementia, which was also extremely painful for me to cope with. The woman who stood by me, and my burdened self, every day. When I met Rhoda I was just a fragile boy trying to figure life out; she helped me become the resilient man I am today.

Over the last 20 years, I have given over 100 talks to schools, football clubs and many large organisations about my experiences in the Holocaust. I was awarded a British Empire Medal from Queen Elizabeth II for dedicating my life to educating others.

Within the last ten years, I have been back to Auschwitz twice: once with my son David and another time with my daughter Judy and granddaughter Lia, both times through the organisation March of the Living.

I celebrated my 90th birthday last year with my four children, six grandchildren and four great-grandchildren (with another one on the way).

As I look back on my life post-Holocaust, I am very thankful to the late Queen and to this country, England, for allowing me and my brother to set up home here. I came with nothing and worked very hard to create a loving and fruitful life for my wife and children. Please G-d, I hope to continue (for myself, my family and loved ones) to always be blessed with health and happiness.

COMMENTS

Chief Rabbi Sir Ephraim Mirvis KBE
Words cannot adequately encapsulate my admiration for you and everything you do. May Hashem's blessings be with you always!

Daniel Carmel-Brown, CEO, Jewish Care
Ivor's account of survival is tragic and moving but his strength shines through. He continues to inspire us all and we are so honoured that he has kindly chosen to donate some of the proceeds from the book to Jewish Care, where Ivor is a much-loved member of our Holocaust Survivors' Centre and our Selig Court Retirement Living apartments.

Olivia Marks-Woldman OBE, CEO, Holocaust Memorial Day Trust
I'm delighted that Ivor's experiences will be shared in this book for audiences yet to come.

Karen Pollock MBE, CEO, Holocaust Educational Trust
It's so important that we know and preserve Ivor's extraordinary testimony. Everyone should read this!

Michael Newman OBE, CEO, The Association of Jewish Refugees

Despite his harrowing childhood and the destruction of his family at the hands of the Nazis, and their accomplices in Hungary, Ivor Perl's compelling story is a restoration of faith in humanity. Hate has not consumed him. In this engaging account of his life, Ivor details his journey from childhood, surviving the unimaginable, to building a new life in a new country. His eyewitness testimony of his deportation to, and incarceration in, Auschwitz is the antidote to Holocaust denial and distortion. In parallel to this important educational resource, he inspirationally regularly summons the courage to revisit his past so that younger generations can hear his remarkable testimony, and he is a widely admired and respected educator.

Scott Saunders MBE, Founder and Chair, March of the Living UK

Having joined Ivor twice on March of the Living, I find his passion for telling his story to young people is remarkable and inspirational. I remember standing in Birkenau when a group of Chassidim approached Ivor with a Sefer Torah and together they sang. I don't think I will ever forget watching this remarkable scene. Ivor telling his story is the most important thing in passing on the torch of memory.

Jonathan Freedland, Author of *The Escape Artist*

A memorable work of Holocaust testimony by a man who endured unimaginable pain but was not broken. Ivor Perl tells his own extraordinary story, but he also has something precious to teach us about life.

Rachel Riley MBE, Presenter and Campaigner Against Antisemitism

Ivor is an incredible man with a deeply tragic start to life. It's important we learn from it, and him, becoming his witness and preserving the memories of those who should never have been taken from him.

Rabbi Jonathan Wittenberg, Senior Rabbi, Masorti Judaism

I've had the privilege of meeting Ivor Perl BEM many times. One would never imagine from his kind smile and warm presence that he'd known so much trauma. Somehow he has managed in his heart to turn his suffering into kindness – the greatest of all human achievements.

Mark Penney, Head of the Prep School, Solihull School

Ivor Perl's chances of survival were about as close to zero as possible, as they were for so many of his loved ones, and millions of others, who perished at the hands of the Nazis. Yet, somehow, he survived. That is a story in itself, and so too is the extraordinary resilience he summoned to recover from the physical, mental and emotional brutalities he endured at such a young age. This is not a book you start to read and put down; the reader is compelled to follow Ivor's journey and to stay with him, horrified by what he shares, inspired by his fortitude.

Chicken Soup Under the Tree is a history book about the things that people did to other people – to Ivor and his family. If our Holocaust teachings are to have a legacy of compassion, empathy and the right kind of decision-making in the future, we must make it clear that History is not about history, it's about people. Families. Ivor Perl's extraordinary story is one all students should know. They will weep and cheer for him, and we will have done our job.

David Morley, Headteacher, St Michael's School

It was a huge honour for the children from my school to meet Ivor. In a world of truth-twisting and conspiracy, I struggle to fully describe the astonishing impact that Ivor had on them. The children were captivated at hearing the story of Ivor's journey first-hand. Ivor shielded our children from the full horrors of his Holocaust experience at the hands of the Nazis and their collaborators, such is the kind and gentle nature of an inspirational educator.

Ivor's book will be a legacy for many future generations, especially children and young people. *Chicken Soup Under the Tree* is set to become a school library essential and will play a vital role in allowing young people to reflect on the tragic murder of six million Jews.

From the publisher

Samuel de Lange, Project Manager, Lemon Soul

Working with Ivor has been in equal parts humbling and inspiring. I have had to continually remind myself that these aren't words on a page; these things actually happened, and they happened to a child. If they are unbearable to think about, what were they like to experience? But Ivor's life is a testament to the incredible power of the human spirit. I met Ivor for the first time when he was in his 90s, but his impish sense of humour and the twinkle in his eye completely mask his years. It has been a huge personal privilege to help bring Ivor's book to the world, and I am a better person for having met Ivor.

REPTON SCHOOL

To Ivor & Rhoda – it was a privilege to have you both with us.

Thank you so much for coming the other week to speak to our boys. I had an excellent discussion with my U. 6th form discussion group the following week. They were very moved by your talk and felt that you ought to come back next year to speak to the new Upper 6th. Would you be able to? With best wishes, Bob

The letters referenced on page 12.

REPTON SCHOOL

The Old Mitre
Burton Road
Repton
Derbyshire DE65 6FH
Thursday 9th March

Dear Ivor,

Just a personal note to thank you and Rhoda for coming all the way to Repton to honour us with your presence at the School.

Your talk was, quite simply, stunning. To keep 120 children, many of whom were tired at the end of a long day, enthralled, and appalled, was evidence that your simple message came across in the most striking fashion. Your message was simple, and completely appropriate to such an impressionable audience — beware evil.

I don't know how you manage to believe in God any more — my wife, Jan, is unable to and having heard you talk, her own feelings have been confirmed. I do believe in Him, so very deeply — it is such a personal matter. But I think that my own belief is subtle in that I believe that we all (& each) have our own path to pursue in our earthly incarnation. I believe, further, that your own calling, if that is adequate, is to talk about your own experiences in order to warn future generations; however difficult and painful you find it.

I shall never forget your talk — I meant every word when I spoke for the whole audience — that it was a great privilege to be there — thank you for being so brave.

Please give my thanks and my best wishes to Rhoda — it was wonderful to see you both again.

With my kindest regards,

Jim

JEWISH CARE

Jewish Care is the leading provider of care and community services for the Jewish community in London and the South East. It provides a wide range of specialist support services for older people, including Holocaust survivors and refugees, people living with physical disabilities and ongoing mental health needs. These include residential care homes, Retirement Living schemes, centres for people living with dementia and community centres, JC Presents online community programme, befriending and Meals on Wheels services. We support people living with dementia, MS and Parkinson's together with their families and carers. Jewish Care touches the lives of 10,000 people each week.

Jewish Care is honoured to have been chosen by Ivor as the charity partner for his book and receives £1 for every copy sold.

Find out more about Jewish Care at **www.jewishcare.org**

117

OF THE LIVING UK

March of the Living UK is an extraordinary, unforgettable experience. It is a packed five-day educational journey in Poland, where UK students, young adults and adults join the March of the Living UK team of the best educators and remarkable Survivors to learn about 1,000 years of Jewish life in Poland and the devastation and horrors of the Holocaust. You spend time travelling around Poland, visiting the sites where Jewish life thrived pre-war, where ghettos were formed and, ultimately, where death and mass destruction of the Jewish population took place. The programme culminates in the International March of the Living event, where the UK delegation joins with 10,000 people from countries all around the world to share in a once-in-a-lifetime experience marching the three kilometres from Auschwitz to Birkenau on Yom HaShoah. You can participate in this historic, life-changing event.

To find out more visit **www.marchoftheliving.org.uk**

'I felt an immense sense of pride to be Jewish following the trip. To see everyone coming together in the face of adversity and commemorating our personal history touched me and I feel changed by my experiences.'

A student participant

LEM⊛N SOUL

Lemon Soul is a campaigns-based publisher, focused on books that have an important message. We partner our titles with relevant charities, helping to raise money and awareness for great causes.

Amazing books can come from anywhere in the world and be on any topic. We are happy to consider all submissions – please contact hello@lemonsoul.com.

Lemon Soul was founded in memory of the fantastic author, and our dear friend, Jonny Zucker.

Find out more about Lemon Soul at **www.lemonsoul.com**

More from Lemon Soul

Get the Children Out: Unsung Heroes of the Kindertransport

By Mike Levy

In aid of Safe Passage

Mike Levy shines a light on the courageous deeds of 22 women and men who transformed the lives of the Kindertransport and other refugees.

In 1938, when the British government refused to act and those around them turned a blind eye, these heroic individuals took it upon themselves to orchestrate one of the greatest life-saving missions the world has ever seen.

Until now the compelling accounts of these extraordinary rescue missions have remained untold.

Mike Levy is a researcher for the US Holocaust Memorial Museum and the Association for Jewish Refugees, an educator with the Holocaust Education Trust and Chair of The Harwich Kindertransport Memorial and Learning Trust.

Available from lemonsoul.com and Amazon